MIDDLE-AGED ADMAN

Ernie Fladell
turned on with pot, tuned into Truth and Beauty in Village crash pads and coffee houses, dug the uptown West Side bars and shared a summer of insight with his guide, co-author and nephew, Richard Lorber.

THE GAP
is his story.

COLUMBIA DOCTORAL STUDENT

Richard Lorber
infiltrated the advertising stratosphere, the martini-oiled groupthink within the carpeted walls of Madison Avenue. He savored $50 luncheons, scrutinized high-powered business transactions and sat in on BLOW-UP-style modeling sessions with his guide, co-author and uncle, Ernie Fladell.

THE GAP
is his story.

". . . entirely too uncomfortable. Undeflected in its honesty, the book is a testimony that the gap is genuine."
Kansas City Times

". . . the book accomplishes its purpose. It has brought two people, and maybe even two generations, closer together through understanding." *Hartford Times*

Other Recent SIGNET Books You'll Enjoy

THE GAP

by Richard Lorber
and Ernest Fladell

A SIGNET BOOK

Published by The New American Library

Library of Congress Catalog Card Number: 68-18550

This is an authorized reprint of a hardcover edition published by McGraw-Hill Book Company.

THIRD PRINTING

SIGNET TRADEMARK REG. U S. PAT OFF AND FOREIGN COUNTRIES;
REGISTERED TRADEMARK—MARCA REGISTRADA
HECHO F. CHICAGO. U. S. A.

*SIGNET BOOKS are published by
The New American Library, Inc.,
1301 Avenue of the Americas, New York, New York 10019*

FIRST PRINTING, JANUARY, 1969

PRINTED IN THE UNITED STATES OF AMERICA

I'm a forty-two-year-old husband, father, businessman. I'm politically moderate and bald. The guy I'm going to live with this summer is twenty and has long hair.

My name is Ernest Fladell. His name is Richard Lorber. I like my friends to call me Ernie. He doesn't like anyone to call him Richie except me, and that is only because I've been doing it for so long.

We're uncle and nephew and we're friends, or at least we are as this book begins. I don't condescend to Richie and he doesn't put me down. We have never tried to act each other's ages or lead each other's lives. In fact there's hardly anything that we have in common except our determination to keep our unusual friendship intact despite the strains of the twenty-two years that separate us.

From the time Richie was thirteen and started traveling to high school in Manhattan from his home an hour and a half away in Rockaway Beach, he began to spend a great deal of time at our home. We then lived in Greenwich Village and he was going to the High School of Music and Art. Before he graduated and was accepted as a student by Columbia University, we had moved to the Upper West Side and so close to his school that it was almost ridiculous for him to travel three hours a day when he could so easily sleep over at our place.

At first, before he became my friend, he was merely a great kid to have around and a wonderful babysitter. And I know he thought I was "cool."

It was during this period, before he grew into his

own apartment and very private life, that Richie and I started telling each other things. We have talked a thousand hours together. And even, these past few years, when Richie began to think of me as "warm" rather than "cool," he still stopped by frequently for long visits and intimate conversations, often stunning me with his intellect and hipness.

These days, the more we talk, the more we know that we're a generation apart on almost everything. We're fascinated with the problem of how to get through to each other. And so I was delighted when Richie asked if he could save a few months' rent by moving in with me this summer while my wife and children were away at the beach. Not only did I happily agree, I capriciously suggested that we try to write about it, and Richie responded with serious enthusiasm.

It is now the beginning of the fourth week in June 1967. I have left my family in Fire Island and returned to the jarring noiselessness of an empty seven-room apartment. Richie's twenty-year-old possessions silently strewn about my thirteen-year-old son's bedroom have added impact to the strange quiet. I now begin to understand, as I'm sure does Richie, the implications of our naïve bargain. I begin to understand that we will be imprisoned together in these pages until September sets us free.

I often feel that Ernie's life is so set and stable that he can have little conception of the other possibilities of existence for a middle-aged man. I had just come back from the West End Bar where I was having an interesting conversation with some of my student friends and an older man who was introduced to us all by one of my friends at the table. He was short and chubby and partly bald; he wore denim pants and a loose polo shirt around which hung a small colorful ceramic doll on a cord of woven gold threads. He had taken LSD the evening before for the first time and had never previously worn such an absurd necklace. When he first joined us and offered to buy us all beers I rashly assumed he must be some sort of odd character attempting to win our collective favor, which didn't bother me one way or the other. Soon I found myself in a fascinating conversation with him about LSD, pot, drugless psychic experiences, and our shared idea of the conscious commitment one must make to live in "reality" after experimenting with certain drugs. He was a sad, quiet-mannered person with a slight lisp; I felt very warmly toward him as I realized that he too was groping for some kind of direction in his life. I felt that we communicated easily and actively with each other, and I made no distinction in my mind between him and my twenty-year-old friends at the table.

When he left our table he seemed incredibly happy. He said he was going home to rethink all of his thoughts about himself and his life, which he felt compelled to do after the ecstatic and monumental experience of the night before. After his departure I was greatly surprised to learn that he was at least forty-five years old and came to the West End Bar for the determined purpose of making contact with younger people, among whom he seemed to feel so completely comfortable. I believe that he actually was going to rethink and recast certain elements in his life. I also think he listened very seriously to the things an anonymous twenty-year-old student had to say, and may very well try some of the experiments in expanded consciousness that I suggested. I suppose this feeling about his candor and openness prompted my disbelief about his age.

I came back to my uncle's apartment. I was surprised to find the door only half locked; sure enough, Ernie was back from the weekend with his family at their summer home on Fire Island.

I remember his wife Judy possessively asserting that Ernie would not be back until Monday morning in answer to the question I had addressed to my uncle as to whether or not we could begin work on the book Sunday night.

On the straw couch in the hall as I entered the apartment a note confirmed Ernie's presence: *Rich: Willard called about 11:15 Sunday. E.*

When I read the note I was amused that Ernie had then already met by telephone the friend I had been planning formally to introduce to him at a later date. Willard is unequivocal in his contempt for Madison Avenue, and his confrontation with Ernie I hoped would become part of a chapter of our book. But the chapter began automatically with Willard's phone call; the book was writing itself.

As I put down Ernie's note, in my mind many thoughts converged in an instant: his wife Judy's possessive remark, Ernie's static and respectable role as husband and father, my confused and experimenting forty-five-year-old acquaintance, Ernie's telephone conversation with his yet unknown adversary, my uncle searching for an escape, home unexpectedly on Sunday night to begin writing a book.

I can no longer think of "my Uncle Ernie" as a constant factor of invariable stability.

For a few years I've been able to tell Ernie about my drug experiences. His commitment to open-mindedness and conviction to understand my generation allowed him privileged communication as far as I was concerned. I suppose at times I abused my freedom of expression. I knew that he could not condone the use of pot publicly, but was compelled to listen to whatever I chose to tell him because of the nature of our friendship; just his attentive consideration of the pleasures of pot as I related them implied a kind of tacit acceptance. I wonder if Ernie felt hypocritical when comparing his public and private stands on the question of pot. Because he basically respects me and will suspend immediate judgment on anything I do, he was forced to be sympathetic in private to something he had to disavow publicly. One summer, as a trustee of the major community on Fire Island, it was his responsibility to support the law and crusade against the use of pot. Ernie is caught between his primary role in what he calls "The Establishment" and the role I cast upon him as an anti-Establishment "subversive," or at best as my confidant. It is in this dual sense that Ernie could finally try pot for himself. "Turning on" was a legitimate experiment for this book—which is, after all, a creative effort (and nothing can be more "Establishment" than the cliché of creativity)—and at the same time the cause of objective experimentation is a mere excuse for something Ernie has for some time wanted to do. Even if my lurid descriptions did not in themselves arouse his interest, I am sure that his basic cultural curiosity sufficed.

So Ernie agreed to try pot, for the book. As we became involved in even the preliminary stages of writing Ernie felt closer to the source of a new experience and displayed what seemed to me a burning anxiousness to smoke. The very premise of writing a book created an insular situation in which Ernie became free to do whatever he really wanted to do, in the same way a "happening" can happen only because of its premise as a creative action. Soon Ernie's desire to "turn on" took precedence over all the other experiences we had planned to share and became our first concrete mutual indulgence.

The question is what is it going to be like in a few years when the kids who are experimenting with pot now become parents? In effect, their children will be born into a pot culture; there'll be psychedelic families. The scene now is that the parents feel personally threatened by their seemingly rebellious children because they are illegally experimenting with pot. Yet legality is not the major concern. I believe that parents are curious, even envious, of this experience but can't risk trying it for fear of condoning what they originally condemned (in ignorance). Now the children born of my generation will have an obvious precedent for smoking pot. What do you think about that?

You're talking as though pot will have a use as widespread as alcohol in my generation. You mean the sort of social drinking, the cocktail before dinner the kids of today see in their own homes? And instead of saying, when Johnny gets old enough, "Let him have a little wine at dinner," they'll give him a drag on their reefer. Do you see this happening?

I see this happening very definitely, perhaps not at dinner, but while the family is listening to music. I think it would be very good. But all of this seems to be hypothetical. Any parents who smoke pot in front of their kids are making it known to the whole neighborhood and would be busted in a week.

Hypothetical or not, I think you've raised more than

11

one question. We are comparing pot to the widespread use of alcohol. Just how many of you out there are smoking pot? Are you telling me that your entire generation is on it?

In the first place, none of my generation is *on* pot. Some of us *take* it. Just your use of the term *on pot* is the vestige of your belief that it is addictive. This to me seems typical of the misinformed middle-aged. And you have to be misinformed if you haven't taken it. But to answer your question: I would say that only a minority do smoke pot. This minority is concentrated in certain areas, and to those who belong to such a group they feel like a majority. I will not deny the exclusive insularity of taking pot.

Would you say that these are the intellectual élite?

Do you think I'm an intellectual?

To me anyone who uses a phrase like "exclusive insularity" is an intellectual.

I hate to miss the chance of establishing myself as part of an intellectual élite, but today the connotations of taking pot are vague. Ten years ago the person who smoked pot was a beatnik and almost by definition an intellectual, but today pot is no longer so esoteric.

Well, just for the hell of it let's see if I can get an answer I can really understand. Say you have ten friends. How many smoke pot?

Eight or nine of them. Close friends.

And how about not-close friends? Maybe people you meet at a party. How many kids there would admit to you that they're on pot from time to time?

Assuming they've taken it at least twice. . . .

Well, you know this is not exactly the Harris Poll. Just give me an educated guess.

I'd say six or seven out of ten.

Yet you say that only a minority of the kids are smoking.

These people are all my friends. The pot scene is very inbred. It seems that everybody who smokes pot knows someone else who smokes pot. We don't know about the others who don't. But I can't believe that it's really widespread. I just think it's a majority of a minority.

Well, in that case I don't think you're going to ever get it legalized.

Unless my friends become senators.

Then they and their kids can sit around of an evening smoking pot and listening to music. I hope I live to see the day that bill is introduced in Congress.

At the moment Richie is in the kitchen cooking a steak for our supper and I'm here at the typewriter trying to say why I'm going to smoke pot tonight for the first time in my life. Pot—marijuana—probably in twenty years it'll be all nicely packaged with cellophane, government tax stamps and all. Filter-tipped, mentholated, king-sized pot, in packages of twenty. But today it is taboo. "Tea" they used to call it. Only the jazz musicians smoked it in the old days, especially drummers. Now, it seems, almost every kid over sixteen and almost nobody over forty has tried it.

They say it's the first step to drug addiction. They say it's harmless. They say it's a better, healthier high than you get from liquor. They say it makes you nauseous. They say. They say. All I know is I don't know.

I've seen people smoke pot and they were weird. The stuff smelled bad to me and looked bad and I never wanted any. What I want is to know what it has got that makes these kids so sure of it and themselves. I mean that nice little girl next door and that clean-cut boy down the block—and my nephew; and my own kids and yours, sooner than we think.

There was a lot of talk last night and a lot of questions about my generation's willingness to experiment; expanded consciousness, tuning in, grooving, and a lot of other stuff I'm vague about. Experiment! I'm willing. If it's good enough for a fifteen-year-old Shelly or Shirley, it's good enough for me. I'll let you know how I make out.

I smoked it.

14

Now what I'm about to tell you is common knowledge for about nine out of ten college freshmen. They're not saying anything to you about it because, in the first place, they don't trust you. In the second place, they wouldn't waste their breath.

"So what's new in school?"

"Oh, nothing much, Dad, except Richie. You know my friend Richie."

"Yeah, nice smart boy Richie."

"Yeah, well, Richie turned me on today."

"That's nice. Was it fun?"

"You know, it sort of expanded my consciousness."

"Well, that's what a father works for, to see his son get a good education. You hear that, Judy? Richie expanded Matthew's consciousness today."

"That's nice."

Or else:

"Turned you on? You mean *pot*? What are you, a bum? A hippie? I'll call a cop and have that crummy pusher arrested."

"But Dad, let me explain."

"Explain? Explain? What is there to explain? My son is a dope addict and he wants to explain. What are you trying to do? Kill your mother? This is what I get for giving you everything. . . ."

So naturally the kids won't tell you.

And the hip writer won't tell you, not in words you can understand. He'd be stripped of his torn blue denim shirt and drummed out of the underground if he were so uncool as to describe anything so mundane except in the abstract. But I'm a forty-two-year-old businessman and I'll tell you.

It's not bad.

It expanded my consciousness, no kidding. Now I know what it means. I listened to music and heard it like never before. I walked down the street aware of every stretch of my leg muscle. I felt relaxed, benign. Pleasantly buzzed, but not drunk. Time stood still. I thought a lot of thoughts. I examined little sensations minutely. That's called grooving. While I was high and sipping a little brandy, which tasted better than I remember it tasting before, I wrote this:

> Sudden revelation: Pot doesn't make me lustful. And isn't that what I've always thought it would do? Maybe it's because so often, when I drink, I drink to let go. The kids are on an entirely different kick. Sex isn't the object, nor is the ability to let go. They have both in reasonably good supply. Their groove is to feel more, see, taste, hear, enjoy more. The kids are hedonistic; we're puritanical.

The precautions not to get caught brought me down. I felt very young and foolish, especially as the stuff came out of hiding like it was the *Spicy Detective* magazine I used to stash under my mattress when I was fourteen.

Then came the ritual of preparing the water-cooled hookah with two mouthpieces (no waiting). A ketchup bottle filled with ice-cold water served as the base and the pipe itself was an Oriental-looking affair that fitted into the top of the bottle. Richie explained as he carefully pricked holes in the tinfoil which would hold the marijuana that this was the most pleasant and comfortable way to smoke pot. Cool!

I insisted that I wanted to try a reefer, since I had seen them smoked with much hissing and coughing and the whole process seemed most unpleasant, uncomfortable, and stupid. An experiment is an experiment. So he rolled a little tea, which smelled mildly aromatic, in straw-colored cigarette paper, twisted both ends, then put the whole thing in his mouth to wet it so it would burn slower. Very unsanitary. I had always thought that college kids picked up mononucleosis from kissing. Now I know it's from passing reefers back and forth. The reason is that one has to hold the smoke in as long as possible so it can enter the bloodstream. Meanwhile all that expensive pot will burn up. Two or more on a reefer is the economical way. Waste not—want not. And they say that the kids of today don't know the value of a dollar!

I asked Richie how long he had been smoking.

"Since I was seventeen, when I entered college."

"How often?"

"Maybe once every three or four weeks. Only when I am sure I have no work to do. I save it as a treat. I really love it."

Incidentally, he has never smoked anything else.

"Where do you get it?"

"Oh, from a friend. There's always someone who knows someone."

"How much does it cost?"

"From fifteen dollars to twenty-five dollars an ounce, depending upon the quality of the pot and the person who sells it. And an ounce lasts a fairly long time."

"What do we do now?"

"First I have to tune you in."

I said, "I have to *turn* you in."

Very funny. Anyhow, I finally learned what *tune in* and *turn on* really meant. Very simple. He tuned me in. It was an orientation lecture. He told me not to expect to feel high as with liquor; that I should try to listen for things—small things, the feel of a breeze, a special effect in the music coming from the stereo, the creak of my knee as I moved.

Come on, Richie, who are you kidding?

He explained terms like *grooving* and *stoned*. He told me how to puff the reefer. And I found out why all the sucking and hissing and sputtering and coughing. Too much of a drag of the acrid stuff grabs you in the throat. So you suck in open-mouthed in short little puffs to mix in as much air as you can. Then I learned why the constipated look I had seen on the few reefer smokers I had witnessed. As I said before, you've got to hold in the smoke as long as you can so it can enter into the bloodstream. It was no fun smoking that reefer. But I got the message.

After a while we tried the hookah pipe. I didn't

know how to puff it and at first got no smoke. But Richie, ever generous, wasted a little pot to see to it that I got my proper share. He got stoned very fast. He told me that just a few puffs turns him on and that past experiences of intense awareness remained and kept building.

He was happy as a lark and said some funny, irrelevant things. I was high but not really feeling what I was supposed to feel and he kept asking me to try things like walking across the carpet barefoot and to concentrate on little sounds. Still so much nonsense. It was just a nice pleasant buzz like I get from one and a half very cold martinis in very good company.

Then I leaned back and listened to the music. I don't know what it was, but how I heard it! I heard everything. It seemed to take forever but I didn't care. And didn't care when it was over.

Suddenly I wanted to go for a walk. I said that maybe all the ritual, tuning in, listening hard and so on would make me hear what I heard if all I did was just drink Scotch.

We went. We walked and we walked and we walked and we walked and we walked. I looked at the street sign on Broadway. We had come about five blocks. It seemed like two miles. I became acutely aware of tension in my calves, not unpleasant, and I also knew that it was the tension I have always felt anytime I walk. It was twenty-two blocks to the West End Bar at 115th Street; it took twenty minutes by my watch, two hours by my head. I saw everything that moved on that street with amazing peripheral vision. I seemed to hear sounds from all directions, clear and loud like a stereo movie.

I felt a little embarrassed and out of place in the bar full of young students and hairy, hipper-than-I characters.

I was dry, very dry and thirsty. I drank two steins of beer. The cold hurt my throat. It felt good.

Richie tried to introduce me to a friend and then forgot and left me standing there with my forty-two-year-old face hanging out. They looked at me like I was an old queer. I didn't care. We sat down and ate the saltiest goddam potato chips going. Richie says if I tried them today they wouldn't taste so salty. But we were able then to convulse ourselves with the idea that they sold especially salty potato chips to make you drink more beer. We spent a lot of time trying to make the chips and the beer come out even . . . finally finishing the last gulp and the last chip at the same time.

A nice kid with a beard sat down at our table, a friend. Richie told him that he, Richie, had just turned on his uncle, me. This started a long conversation about how it feels. That seems to be what it's mostly or all about for these kids. Not a bad hangup. Another kid came over with lots of hair. He was wearing a picture button. I took a look. "Cassius," I said. "Muhammad," he said. "Oops, pardon me."

Then there was some more inconsequential conversation. For a change I didn't talk too much. Greatest thing for me about this high was my ability to keep quiet and ignore conversational leads for long periods of time.

I knew I was quite high—in the language of pot, "stoned." I remembered how when deep in my cups I have looked in the mirror of a washroom and grinned at my reflection and have actually talked to myself: "You're drunk, you silly bastard." Now I went to the john and deliberately looked into the mirror there. Looking back was a perfectly normal face, recognizably my face, unchanged and unaware of the high in my mind. I washed it, dried it, brought it back to the table where some delightful conversation was going on, none of which I bothered to hear.

Finally, I told Richie I was tired. We left, got a cab, came home, and I went to bed. I slept well. So that's my whole pot experiment . . . almost all Jekyll and no Hyde.

Before we "turned on" I asked him whether he truthfully wished to find that pot was overplayed and rather insignificant as an experience or if he wanted to find himself amazed by a new and unique feeling that was very pleasurable. At first he admitted that he was hoping it would all prove to be a fraud, a high not unlike alcoholic drunkenness. Ernie was here showing his persistent defensiveness about his "respectable" role when confronted with a test of acceptance of my scene. But as I set up my hookah—and I admit I theatrically extended the ritual of preparation—Ernie became almost thrilled at the nearness of the experience and voluntarily told me that he was really hoping to get stoned, to find that pot was different.

That Ernie's objective, experimental attitude was fused with a genuine desire for a new kick became again clear to me before we smoked. When I told him we would be using a hookah he seemed somewhat disappointed. He wanted to smoke the prototype of a reefer just like you read about in books or hear about on television. It seems that some twenty years ago Ernie missed an opportunity to take a couple of puffs of what he called a "stick of tea"; he was suspicious of the thing's appearance and "turned off" by its acrid smell. So I rolled a joint for Ernie and recreated the moment he may for twenty years have regretted denying; but we mainly used the water-cooled hookah, which is far more civilized. (I don't smoke tobacco and never have. I therefore object to the discomfort of a marijuana cigarette basically on the ground that it is a cigarette. Also I do not enjoy the hot, voluminous smoke of a joint; a water pipe refines and cools the smoke. Once, however, I was going to smoke a "roach," which is the butt of a joint in a regular cigarette; I tapped out some of the tobacco from the tip of the cigarette, inserted the "roach," and lit up. I soon found that I preferred pot to tobacco purely on the basis of comparative smoke. As I drank deeply the fumes of the marijuana all was fine, but as I inhaled the beginning of the tobacco I nearly choked.)

As we smoked, Ernie had difficulty inhaling properly, although he smokes almost two packs of Camels every day. It is one thing to inhale and exhale; it is something else to inhale and keep it in for a time as one must do with pot. Ernie was gulping the smoke and having difficulty holding his breath. It would have been advisable to do breathing exercises before beginning with him. I was savoring the smoke in my throat and lungs; I am favorably conditioned to what is, I guess, an objectively unpleasant feeling. But Ernie got high. And I was more stoned than usual since I was generous in the portions I served to my neophyte uncle; my hookah has two breathing tubes and we communally shared the pot in the pot.

It's not enough to just turn someone on; Ernie had to be tuned in as well. Most people are disappointed with their initial pot experience basically because they don't know where the experience is. A pot high is not like an alcohol one; one doesn't feel as if twenty pounds of damp laundry had been dropped on one's head. Pot is quiet. It is a droning dust inside your brain. It drifts in a corner and each person must find where it is in himself; you must sniff for it, feel for it, listen for it. I suggested that Ernie gently rub two fingertips together and imagine the clatter of their grating surfaces. I suggested that Ernie listen for the sound of the hammer striking the anvil inside his inner ear. I suggested that he just listen to the stereo sound of the Rolling Stones, which I was playing. As he intently listened I turned the balance knob from one speaker completely to the other, back and forth; I then told him to close his eyes and watch the sound move in acoustical space from one side of the room to the other.

Ernie now felt that he was high and was fascinated by the fact that he was not drunk. He could not believe that pot was such a "mild" high, as he called it. He was, I am sure, expecting a dulling physical effect. Although I had told him many times that pot lives in the mind, not in the body, he had previously refused to understand such a separation. Pot makes you aware of the mind as an entity apart from the head. If you expect to feel something in your head or stomach or toes you'll never know you're high. The only physical sensation is living an illusion; heightened awareness is feeling nothing new as something new. That's why you can groove on only what you've got in you to groove on. Everyone discovers his own high in his own way. I knew if I tried to direct Ernie that I would only be imposing my own awareness on him; since we were different people he would have to find for himself what it meant to be stoned. I could only roll hints.

After turning on, listening to music, taking a long walk, and sitting in the West End Bar, Ernie had enough. His initiation was over and he wanted to go to sleep. We would both write about our experiment the next day. What bothered me was Ernie's attitude. He burned some pot one time and acted as if he knew what it was all about; he believed he could now dispense with the whole matter as a harmless, rather pleasurable experience and go away with a substantial insight into my generation. Ernie thinks he can get a bird's-eye view of the labyrinth by sitting on a cloud of smoke. But if he doesn't get lost in the maze he'll never know what it's all about. Pot is a learning experience and each time one turns on the effect is amazingly accumulative. Many of my friends consider pot to be an experience of sacred depth; Ernie found that it was "not bad." I want him to try it again. I want him to know the sensation of tuning himself in. I want to watch him find his own groove.

Many young people are condemned for experimenting with pot; they are said to be rebellious and irresponsible, seeking new kicks. But they don't have the excuse of writing a book. My experimenting, middle-aged uncle is the caricature of any teen-ager turning on for the first time, only the kick of being stoned is respectably displaced by the kick of reporting it. Ernie is less turned on by the genuine experience than by his messianic duty to inform the grounded middle-aged.

As I reflect upon what I have written I realize something that may be obvious. I introduced Ernie to pot, I turned him on, and I wanted him to get high. But now that he claims to know the experience I feel somewhat resentful; it is as if he had crashed a very private party I was having with myself. I can no longer condescend to him about the mysteries of pot; my cultural insulation burned away in his throat.

Ernie left Friday morning at around ten-thirty for the Island. That same Friday, my year-long girlfriend left me to begin a year of study in Iceland. I went that afternoon to the Wildenstein gallery with a female acquaintance I had met the previous summer in Florence; there was an exhibit of some excellent Renaissance paintings shown as a benefit for flood-damaged Florence. In the evening I went to the Met to see Hindemith's *Mathis der Mahler,* an opera about the sixteenth-century German painter Matthias Grünewald; a rich friend took me to see it. Later at his apartment we drank French apéritif and German beer, ate fried clams, and talked.

Saturday morning I was feeling very lonely. I wandered up to Columbia. In a shop that sells psychedelic accessories, a headshop, I bumped into a girl I knew. I asked if she knew of any parties; I was desperately craving a party, which is to say I was craving a girl. She told me of a party in the East Village, adding that it would be a freak-out and that she had to contact a friend to get the address. I told her that I wasn't interested in tripping on acid at this time but that I would be delighted to turn on. She said that there would be a lot of pot as well as LSD; she said I should call her in a couple of hours. I then went over to the Columbia lawn and sat on the grass, thinking about things for about twenty-five minutes; opening a book I began to read a scholarly account of the Mithraic Mysteries, my current interest. Tiring of the bugs on the lawn, I rambled toward the West End Bar and a glass of iced tea;

24

there were still thirty-five minutes left in the "couple of hours" after which I had been instructed to call about the party. But I again bumped into the girl, this time in a record store a block before the West End. She was buying the new Beatles album. She waved to me, I went into the store, and she invited me back to her apartment to hear the album after I heavily hinted that it would be my pleasure to do so. At the apartment we listened and finger-painted. She and a friend had rediscovered finger-painting; this was the true psychedelic art; together we did a painting in green, yellow, and blue and one in black. The smell of the jellied paint reminded me of the fourth grade.

Her record player was like a child's phonograph; it was a shame to spoil a new record with a bad needle and so I asked if she would like to hear her new record and any others on my stereo. She agreed; I told her I had some pot as well. Fortunately her party informant was not at home. We stopped at his apartment on 111th Street; he had no telephone and the note she left earlier asking for the address was still posted in the same place.

We walked to 93rd Street. I was tired and feeling depressed. For some reason the sounds of the street were droning in my ears and the humid late-afternoon mist burned my eyes, or it may have been the fumes of passing cars. Upon entering the building I proudly signaled to the young, friendly Puerto Rican doorman; I was pleased with my catch but somewhat annoyed that the same doorman would not be on duty the next morning, Sunday, to observe us leaving the building. I showed her the apartment, put on some records, and excused myself to go to the bathroom. I had to brush my teeth; at her apartment she had served me tuna fish and anchovies, both of which I was still tasting and I assumed were on my breath. I couldn't bear the thought of turning off a girl with my tuna-fish breath.

At first, when I reentered the living room, she was sitting in the armchair opposite me. I explained that she could not appreciate the total stereo effect unless she was centered in between the speakers (and, after all, that was why we were at my uncle's apartment). She then understandingly seated herself close beside me on the couch. By the end of a Rolling Stones album I was comfortably kissing her; it would, I suppose, have been better to start at the beginning of the fourth band, but passion is undeniably spontaneous. She lowered her body and stretched out her legs; she responded to me throughout a song and a half with only her lips but I knew that her thighs were passively awaiting my initiative. But somehow the seduction was without conviction; I was indifferent.

Finding myself still quite thirsty after the tuna fish and anchovies, I politely offered her a glass of iced pineapple juice, all that I could find in the refrigerator. I felt ridiculous serving her in the nude but at least I was able to quench my own thirst; to extend the absurdity I apologized for not having served the drink in a pineapple shell with a bamboo straw. That amused her and I sat down, crossing my legs.

I then suggested that we turn on.

Since I broke the water glass container of my hookah I've had to improvise with an empty Heinz ketchup bottle, the only bottle with a nozzle into which I can firmly fit my rubber plug. We each sucked on our respective tubes (my hookah has two coming out of the plug, allowing us to share the pot). We both quickly got high. I then coaxed her body to the hard carpeted floor. My favorite Rolling Stones song had begun, the eleven-minute number called "Going Home," and I was determined to indulge a long-subdued fantasy. She was wet and the music also seemed wet.

During the next hour and a half we sank our potted minds into other sounds. During the latest Beatles album we shared another orgasm, this time in a vividly contorted position. The music finished and we fell asleep on the couch. We roused each other in discomfort at 6 A.M. and went into the chilly air-conditioned bedroom. It was a luxury to sleep with blankets during the summer, but I was too dazed with dreams to be aware of anything but the gulp of a mattress.

The telephone raped my sleep at ten. I shook a glance at the body pressed to mine and lifted the receiver to hear my mother's packaged voice. She seemed distant and I barely stirred when she matter-of-factly stated that I had received a 1-A classification from my draft board. I was awake enough not to be confused but tired enough not to care; I thanked her and announced that I was going back to sleep. I turned over, saw two eyes open, closed mine and fell back into a dream. Mother on the telephone again tickled me awake at ten-thirty; she was sending me the draft forms; she wanted my zip code. I was now fully awake. I realized that her call may have crippled my future. In September I was to begin a five-year fellowship at Columbia University to get a Ph.D. in art history; that suddenly became a fantasy.

I hung up and took a long, thoughtful shower; I told the girl to use, if she cared to, the other bathroom. We didn't have much to say to each other. The living room looked like the scene of pure evil. I made some espresso coffee, put on Beethoven's Trio, Opus 1, No. 1, and evaded conversation. That afternoon we took a short walk and went to a couple of movies at a local theater; I didn't notice who the doorman was as we walked out of my uncle's building. I abruptly left her after the films, excusing myself with the promise of a call. I was expected for dinner at the house of an older married friend; I was anxious to reveal the new drama in my life and to seek sympathy from him and his attractive wife, but more deeply I was too scared not to dramatize; I couldn't quite bear the sudden imminence of war and death. What I felt most on leaving the theater was that I did not want to be alone. Ernie would not be back until the evening of the Fourth of July and this was only the second.

It is about 11:30 P.M. Tuesday, the Fourth of July. I

have just returned after spending four days with my family on Fire Island, expecting to find Richie here ready to go to work. But he isn't home. So I read again some of what we have written. Outside, they're shooting off firecrackers. I had forgotten that this is July 4 and I thought at first crack that I had heard gunshots. Then I kept hearing the shots and remembered the date with relief.

I'm curious to see how we manage to combine our notes and narratives into something intelligible and cohesive. But I'm even more intrigued with the direction this book is taking. The contradictions in my life seem to be shaking him up. Richie writes about me with an analytic fervor that seems to be reversing the roles somewhat. There seems to be an undue emphasis placed on what is admittedly my lack of sophistication concerning pot. As he has said, he will be me, more or less, in about twenty years. And he seems to be trying very hard to fix me in place. The fact that I won't stand still and conform is, I think, a little unsettling.

We talked a little last week about another kind of experiment. And I will try to set it up tomorrow. I wonder what will happen when Richard meets one of my more respectable (his word) clients and finds himself face to face with a real Madison Avenue work situation. If my man is willing, we'll do the whole bit; lunch, conferences, gathering information inside the client's company, working under executive supervision, and trying to come up with just one real ad, fresh, workable, and acceptable. If he is confused about me, wait till he meets some of my contemporaries on their own turf. I am interested in Richie's reaction to the many-faced business world and to men with many experiences behind them and many responsibilities before them, and with conflicting ideas on how to exercise their prerogatives.

About the time I had finished the last few paragraphs Richie came in. We've taken to writing each other little memos within the context of this book, and it was clear to me that he had something to tell me because he was anxious for me to read some pages he had worked on over the weekend. It was all about his having a girl in the apartment, mainly in my air-conditioned bedroom and in my clean sheets all weekend. As pornography it was pretty thin stuff, and the only thing that really grabbed me was an almost casual disclosure that he had just been reclassified 1-A. That was Richie's message to me. The Vietnam war had just written itself into our book.

We had previously decided that we were not going to do anything on Vietnam because you can read Richie's view in *New Left Notes* and mine in *The New York Times*. But now the war was suddenly in my living room, ugly and inescapable.

Richie told me that he was very worried, that he was facing one of the most agonizing decisions of his life. We had both thought that Richie's academic standing and the fact that he had earned a graduate fellowship at Columbia would surely keep him deferred. My reaction was strange. For one irrational moment I couldn't help taking some satisfaction in seeing Richie's smugness shattered and knowing that my nephew would now face some of the experiences, indignities, fears, frustrations, and the loss of momentum that I had suffered when I was eighteen. But this was also my nephew, my sister's boy, my friend. All at once I wanted to cry.

I went to war weak with fear but strong in my pride. Richard has only fear. He may have to fight and die a dirty death for a cause he despises, or rush into a decision that may expatriate him or even jail him. Also, for the first time I realized with piercing keenness this might well be the image of my thirteen-year-old son seven years from now.

Richie will try for a continued deferment, knowing that someone else will have to replace him. He will do this because he believes that no one should fight this war and draft resistance is a form of protest. Failing in his appeals, he can leave the country, or he can accept two years' service in the Armed Forces and take his chances. And the chances are he will survive, hating and resenting every minute of it.

Richie knows I feel he should not leave the country under any circumstances, and this negates any advice or help I can give him, other than my sympathy for his predicament and support for anything he does. Unless you know Richard personally, you will probably never learn what happens to him because this book will be finished before this is resolved. But now the war is with us every minute we spend together.

The other evening I met Richie for dinner near 110th Street, where he told me he was going to take me to a "charming Spanish restaurant." He brought a girl along, to my surprise and delight. I realized how tired I was getting of being in Richie's company only and found myself enjoying a new face to look at, especially a pretty feminine face.

The "charming Spanish restaurant" turned out to be a little luncheonette run by a Spanish family. The peppered steak Richie recommended highly as a "specialty" was very nicely flavored peppers and gristle, and the pink foaming fruit drink he said I must try and which he himself savored tasted of peaches and bananas in the second stages of decay.

The young lady, however, was quite refreshing, especially since she was most intrigued by what I had to say—or at least was very polite. Richie told me later that if I had talked a little less and given her more of a chance, she might have asked me some very pertinent questions which I would have found worth noting for our mutual literary effort. However, I did notice that she didn't wear a brassiere and learned that she did not smoke pot. I was tempted to tell her that she was in a twenty-per-cent minority of Richie's friends.

And she did find her chance to ask me, in the direct way kids ask questions:

"Do you have fears that writing this book will change your life?"

I answered in several thousand ill-chosen words that

31

I was only afraid that writing this book would not change my life.

Later in the conversation she told Richie he was being paranoid when he talked about how his draft board had singled him out for some unknown reason. It struck me that Richie also uses the word *paranoid* very often and I have since observed that his other friends do, too. I don't know precisely what it means in their context, but it doesn't quite link up with my use of *nervous, tense,* or *fearful.* It seems more specifically to relate to any defensive reaction of theirs to someone or something else's threatening behavior, real or imagined. Blowing their cool, so to speak.

I also became aware that these kids don't often use terms like *blowing your cool, up tight, groovy,* expressions you find in profusion in slick magazines and advertisements that pretend to be on the inside of the youth scene. Richie and his friends seem to be very studied in their refusal to talk the language they are supposed to talk. And so at about the time you think you know what they are saying, they have changed the words and the meanings.

About this matter of language, Richie says that one of the big problems between the generations is that we don't think the same things are funny. And I'll admit so far my experiences with Richie haven't been exactly a barrel of laughs, although he may be having one or two privately.

The other night I spent a few hours in the West End Bar again. And, although I have become rather un-selfconscious about my businesslike middle-aged appearance in a place full of disheveled college students, I soon found out I'm a long way from "in."

The West End is not what you'd expect as a campus hangout. Its black formica front features foot-high Old English letters spelling out its name. Inside in the middle is a circular bar with busy, uncommunicative bartenders tending its fifty-foot length. Coming in on

the left is a long cafeteria affair. On the right and all
around at the back are booths and tables served by
waiters in unpressed red Eisenhower jackets, and no
ties. The decor is woody and institutionally modern—
that is to say, bad. But as I stood at the bar waiting for
Richie, I noticed that there was a mixture of plain or-
dinary neighborhood people, and even some of the students were wearing suits and ties.

I must admit that Richie's talk of this place had gotten me a little "paranoid." We had discussed my
clothes the other evening and the fact that the last time
I had appeared there in what I considered casual
clothes, neatly pressed tan chinos and a fresh open-collar shirt, it seemed I had looked a little too summery,
trying a little too hard. I protested that these were always the sort of things I changed into when I got home
at night. The only comfortable clothes I have are
clean. What am I to do? The conversation began to assume ridiculous proportions, which we both realized
after a while, and the subject was dropped.

Still, for this date, where I expected to meet a few of
Richie's closer friends whom I hope I will come to
know better, I mentally reviewed some of the beaten-
up remnants I had hanging in the back of my closet,
thinking that maybe I would try to disguise myself a
little. But I never had a chance because I had forgotten my keys and also had forgotten that I was to meet
Richie at the West End and not at home. So I arrived
in my Brooks Brothers summer worsted, blue button-
down, and paisley tie—fortunately my shoes weren't
shined.

After all that talk about clothes, Richie came in
wearing my new blue-striped polo shirt. It fitted comfortably across his skinny shoulders and around his
twenty-eight-inch waist, and I thought to myself "I
guess I'll never wear that one again," wondering how I
had had the gall to cram my somewhat thicker frame
into a shirt that just fit my nephew.

For a while we played musical booths to find a
smart location, and Richie went over to the cafeteria

for a couple of hamburgers while I called for two steins of beer.

About the time we had finished, several of Richie's friends had drifted in and soon I was surrounded by hairy youths with the usual assortment of beards, mustaches, Veronica Lake hairdos, gold-rimmed glasses out of which peered sweetly innocent young eyes. I had learned my lesson of the other day quite well and muttered back something incoherent to the muted and equally incoherent introductions. At first they ignored me and talked their own kind of gossip and small talk. There was some kind of conversation about horny movies they had seen and were going to see, with one kid describing a recent Bergman picture as the most rock-hard thing he had ever seen. I was lulled into a sense of false security because this was something I could easily understand.

Then out of nowhere one of the kids, whom they called Willard, said in my general direction: "The ad man who got the idea to shave the peach on television says that advertising is subsidized poetry."

I answered this with something brilliantly bland, like "You know how it is with some guys in advertising." And I realized that my credits as the president of a small advertising agency had preceded me. There was nothing much more about that for a while, and then one of the kids asked me point-blank how come I don't do a clever ad for peace in Vietnam. I said I would be glad to if anyone asked me to and paid for it, although I would like it to run in the *Peking Evening Star* as well as *The New York Times*.

Then somebody said "Would you take the Dow account?"

"You bet," I said.

"Even though they make napalm?" he asked.

I asked him how he was going to school and who was paying for it. "My father's bosses' money" he answered.

"Supposing your father worked for Dow selling

Saran Wrap. Would that mean you would quit school in protest?"

One of the other kids said: "Oh! that's hardly fair."

But another one said it was so fair and somehow in the ensuing discussion I got off the hook for a while.

Then someone asked me if I was defensive about advertising and I said "No, only when I allow my agency to do bad advertising." I was pushed rather hard on that one and for the only time that evening I tried to get through to them by trying to explain my interest in doing good work. I thought I was making some points by telling them of the new graphics and copy approach we use and how we try to tell it true and then somebody said "But what you're saying is that you're working within the system and trying to improve it. And what we're saying is that the system shouldn't exist at all."

I would have asked him what he wanted to replace it with, but somehow I knew he really had no ideas on that subject. I asked Richie about him later and he explained that this boy was completely apolitical, or rather that he practiced politics of the perverse. Whatever that means.

During most of the conversation I was careful not to say too much or overexplain or be too defensive. I initiated nothing and tried to answer the questions that were put to me with a "yes" or a "no" wherever possible.

At one point a kid asked me: "Why did you go into advertising in the first place?"

I thought back almost twenty years and answered as honestly as I could: "To make a living."

He then said: "That's one of the things I can't understand about you fellows, doing what you do just to make a lot of money."

I said: "I went into advertising to make a living, not to make a lot of money." Even as I said it I knew the phrase *to make a living* could have absolutely no meaning to these children of the affluent society.

"Now," I told him, "even though I make what you

would consider a lot of money, I'm in the advertising business more for the glory." I knew as I spoke that they wouldn't understand. There was no way to explain it to them. Many of my clients, my close personal friends, and even other colleagues in the business don't really understand, so how could I expect comprehension from a group of twenty-year-old students when they hear something as outrageous as an advertising man saying that he does what he does for the glory of it?

Finally conversation drifted off into esoteric areas of academia that mercifully excluded me. Richie tells me that I did well; that his friends will now accept me as I am. But I'm not sure that I accept their ignorance and one-dimensional dogma.

This book is developing a consciousness of its own, complete with a neurosis drawn from the mass of suppressed thoughts which cannot find their way into print. Ernie's experience with pot was the first trauma to be suffered by the infant ego of our manuscript. I expect that repercussions will be felt throughout the work.

Presently I am about to enter Ernie's world. I am to spend a week or two working in his advertising agency, helping to supervise the conception and execution of a series of ads for one of his major clients. This experience may be the book's second trauma.

My intellectual resistance to the business world will have to be somewhat overcome if I am to do an effective job. Ernie has presented the whole situation to me as a kind of challenge. My smugness about the virtue of academic life as opposed to the morality of the business world provokes him to comment on my naïveté. I may well be naïve; I am still a student; I have been sheltered from "real life." I can therefore command my intolerance with impunity; Ernie usually winds up agreeing with me or cajoling my position rather than defending his own. While I use my academic prerogative to criticize business, he, as a representative of business, is trying to determine what could induce me to become part of it. A businessman will make you shoot him in anger only to demonstrate a bulletproof vest which he'll then try to sell you.

I know I've been talking about business abstractly, as if it were some huge amoebic monster; that's partly why I decided to join Ernie's company for a week or two. I wanted to see if I could recognize the dignity he claims for this life; I wanted to see just how the business world piqued me when I was inside looking out. Ernie continually suggests an analogy with his pot experience; he repeats that this introduction into business is his way of turning me on. He claims that I am contemptuous of the business world because I fear that I might like it. He may be correct, but the ultimate question for me is not whether I like business, it is whether I could be in business and like myself.

My first harsh confrontation with Ernie's world was a disorienting fifty-dollar business lunch at a restaurant called The Four Seasons. There were three of us: Ernie, myself, and an executive who was representing the account on which I would be working. The two martinis before lunch washed away my prepared venom; alcoholic pacification must be one of the subversive maneuvers of business, I thought. I had been prepared to attack the irresponsibility of the business community, to blast the two men taking me to lunch with questions and accusations. I wanted to know why there has been so little, if any, organized protest against our country's murderous aggression in Vietnam: the two businessmen with me had admitted their opposition to the war privately but could not take any public stand. Academicians need not be the only ones to bear the burden of public protest; why couldn't a group of influential businessmen at least muster the conviction to put their names on an open letter against the war—some evidently do oppose President Johnson's outrageous policies? Do these business people, the unquestionable "power élite," think that their silence preserves for them an apolitical neutrality? Within the past few years political attitudes have become so polarized around the Vietnam issue that silence can only mean the affirmation of policy—and the business community knows it.

A businessman will shun individual responsibility for his community's corporate silence, yet he will appropriate the individual privileges gained through corporate power. My uncle tells me that it would be unfeasible for him to initiate an open letter or petition against the war in Vietnam; without asking for further explanation, I know that he would not risk alienating politically conservative clients or future clients. I feel that sometime, somehow, somewhere an important representative of the business community must break the ice of silence; but from talking to my uncle and others, that layer of ice seems more like a massive glacier.

Unfortunately, all of these infected political sores became nothing more than well-powdered blemishes on the matte complexion of a very social afternoon. I realized quite a few things about business lunches and business in general. Ernie later confirmed my first conclusion: the most successful business lunch is one where business is barely discussed. Personally I can't imagine how anyone can talk meaningfully or usefully about anything after a couple of martinis on an empty stomach, and yet the consumption of a good quantity of alcohol seems to preface any discussion. (At least when you smoke pot, you don't really care to talk—silence is better than nonsense.)

The official purpose of our luncheon was to begin considering a series of ads my uncle's agency would be doing for this particular client. As a kind of research for this book, I would be entering Ernie's daily world through working with him on that project. Soon after we were seated at the table, the client made it clear that he was not ready to begin even thinking about the ads for at least another two weeks. It suddenly seemed to me that their "business" lunch had become merely a matter of food. But I soon found myself bobbing with the others in a kind of martini daze and I understood that business really couldn't matter even if we had some to try to talk about. It must be a businessman's nightmare actually to have to sell something to a client at such a luncheon.

If it was Ernie's job to talk business, it was my business to talk politics; I had been waiting for just such an opportunity to launch my invective against the business community and ask some pertinent questions in the process. But the setting, atmosphere, and nature of the ensuing discussion displaced my intended business just as the client had displaced Ernie's. Everything was so pleasant; the restaurant was some kind of floating reality—an effect certainly in part attributable to those mollifying martinis. Any serious discussion about anything seemed delicately irrelevant. Once the food was served and my stomach filled and functioning absorbently, I did touch on some of the political matters I had been considering beforehand, but I couldn't get into a crusading spirit and the argument was forensically feeble. Sitting for three hours in one of the most elegant restaurants in New York, eating and drinking, had made all other concerns seem marginal and subsidiary; I was indulging myself in the immediate situation as heartily as my two companions.

Businessmen reward their faith in the absolute value of the present moment with these kinds of luncheons. They create what I now understand to be the positively essential social foundation of any business relationship; the "business deal" is merely an economic superstructure imposed upon this foundation. Business is a kind of game where men who believe in the rules get together to test their skills. The game can exist only in the immediate present because of the nature of these rules; they must at every moment be called into use or challenged. I entered the game with the idea that I could talk about the responsibility of those who play the game to the people who watch it and wait for the outcome. But the game exists for its own sake and only at the moment it is being played. Business can be neither progressive nor reactionary; it can only exist for itself within the circumstances of its day-to-day conditions. *Responsibility* is a term with implications extending into future; this term, I learned, was incompatible with the nature of business because business is the mechanism of immediacies. Although the "business luncheon" may not be a microcosm of the whole business world, it certainly is one of the most recognizable features in any standard caricature.

I can't help being constantly aware of how different is Richie my roommate, my co-author, my critic, from the winning, studious, respectful Richie, my nephew. I certainly must appear as much a stranger to him. In a way he and I have become players in a drama. The more we probe for the truths about us, the more unreal we seem to become to each other. We have recently grown stingy with our opinions, as though neither wants to cue the other in. We seem now only to communicate through the book. At first we said all we had to write. Now we are writing what we have to say. I hope this will change again. I miss the warm comfort of our long rambling Talmudic debates. I can't help feeling that it is Richie and not I who is holding back. He has now ventured into another society. The variety of people and impressions is wide and confusing. He was looking for a structure into which he could fit and found none that he could discern, much less fit into. Like a businessman on the town looking for free love in the East Village, Richie is looking for an immediate glimpse of hostility, confusion or pressure, or greed, or defensiveness, or fear, or obsequity or conniving. Come out, I know you're there. Wait, Richie. It all will come out. What Richie is afraid of is that it will come out in him.

Of course, for any red-blooded intellectual my business poses another threat. The advertising business is very easy to like. The people are fun, and it's a creative challenge. But it's also a rough economic battlefield where time, effort, and ideas are just so much expendable ammunition. Wounded and dying egos are everywhere. I've risked mine every day for the last fifteen years and I've got the scars to prove it. I've also still got my ideals, self-respect, and a lot more to learn.

But, for my money, it's the best game in town. And they feed you pretty good, too.

Richie cannot accept the concept that anything so dependent on existing institutions can leave a man free to think and act as he pleases in private life. Yet all the best businessmen I know are free-thinkers and intellectually curious, knowledgeable, and more interested in making a mark than in making a buck. There are also a lot of frightened, stupid clods around. But so what? They have a right to live, too. Nowhere else could they feel so useful or be so useful to society than from within the buoyant business world. Many of the games businessmen play are for the sake of the clods. Frequently the clods dominate the game and then it gets very disgusting.

What is the game? The same game as the college game or the politics game. The name of the game is "Beat your father at building a better world for your son." Sometimes a businessman thinks he's only out for money. Then he dies and he leaves his money to a college or toward building a library or creating a park. The smarter ones do it while they're alive. Or else their sons will. I don't give a damn what excuses some businessmen give for doing the right things or how every decent thing they do is put down as corporate interest or a play for public favor. If the profit motive is the only motive they'll admit they have for moving the world forward an inch, I say more profit to them. But how can Richie believe any of this? I hardly believe it myself, even though I see it.

I also see the seamy side of business, the sharks who eat the clods, the scavengers who pick the bones. I despise them and the cynics and the hacks and the cowards. But I adore all the movers and the shakers, all the little and big ones. How can I describe all the different sizes and guises in which they come and all the surprising places they're found, and all the disappointments, frustrations, anxieties they must overcome, all the courage they must show and energy they must use to make any one idea they believe in come true? These are some of the best men in the world with the lousiest public relations. Who the hell is Richie to judge their worth?

Richie met a good man at lunch. Did he mistake courtesy and interest for a con job? Did he confuse intelligence with shrewdness? Did he take objectivity for callousness? As I write this I don't know what Richie thought about our deliberately overstated lunch, except that he ate like a horse. Richie was to work on a series of ads for this client, who had been intrigued with the entire experiment and was curious about the new generation's thinking. Very little business was discussed at lunch, except to put the project off for a week and the extending of an invitation to Richie to sit in on a very intimate planning session, usually reserved only for top people at the company. Thereafter, conversation carried through a half-dozen topics, lingering a long while on politics. Later, Richie wanted to know if this was usual. What's ever usual or unusual at a business lunch? It all depends on the mood, the relationship, the need, and who said what to whom about what that morning. The usual thing is to work in our own offices, and the most unusual thing about our lunch was that Richie was there in the first place.

Before the lunch Richie had asked me if he could say anything he wanted to. I told him he could and he did. My business friend, who is about fifteen years more experienced than I, is impressively well-informed, and I enjoyed his handling of Richie's questions, which were almost accusations. I thought Richie would be impressed too, but he was hardly aware of our older companion's intelligent and fair if somewhat careful answers to Richie's questions on a businessman's responsibility regarding the Vietnam war. Richie seemed far more interested in making the questions as hardnosed as possible, taking time out to be fascinated with the tableside ritual of a steak tartare being prepared for my lunch. He later ate half of it in addition to the frog's legs he had ordered. He seemed to be enjoying himself immensely, but later I discovered he despised the fact of his own enjoyment.

On the way back to the office, Richie expressed disappointment that we hadn't really discussed anything specifically related to the reason for the lunch. I've told him before so I didn't tell him again that business and politics don't mix. Richie could have asked questions about our luncheon companion's company and his advertising objectives—and the lunch would have been more productive; instead Richie wanted to know why his corporation was not protesting the Vietnam war.

I wonder what kind of questions he'll ask of the people in my office and how he'll like their answers, especially when it gets down to doing what they're paid for. They'll accept him. But will he accept their help, not knowing that this is the way it's done? He will also be surprised at how difficult it is to crystallize an idea in a few words and simple graphics. That's providing he gets an idea.

The way it's going, he may not get a chance. He came in today, expecting to get started. I suggested he call and set an appointment with our client of the big lunch. But the lunch had worked no magic. There was another postponement. I know Richie is frustrated. As it is he acts as though he's being compromised. His time is much too valuable to waste on such frivolity. Let's get on with it. But business is mindless of individual timetables. It reminds me of the Army. Hurry up and wait. Things have been difficult for me, too, these last few weeks. There's little life in the shop. It's July and nobody seems to want to move on anything.

In order to get something going, I've been doing everything but a rain dance. Next week I think I'll buy a tom tom and wear feathers. All the while, Richie has not been exactly what you'd call a source of comfort and inspiration.

Anyhow, I think our boy had a good time today. He watched me squirm beneath the pressure of a very uncomfortable administrative problem: that is, one of our larger, more sensitive clients being a little long on credit and us being a little short on cash. I thought I handled it beautifully. I don't know what Richie thought. But I'll tell you I could have used a little pat on the back from someone.

Richie also sat in on a meeting in which we were beginning work on ads for a new client. These sessions got pretty abstract and sometimes very nutty. Method advertising. I'm sure Richie couldn't have known what we were talking about, because we didn't either. It's always like that when the page is blank. The problem is to find the problem. Most clients will tell you everything but where it hurts. So, after you've gotten all the information you can find in or out of their company, examine it in the light of what you've been told, and match it with what you know, you hunt around until you touch a nerve. Ouch! That's it. Then all you have to do is execute it and sell it. Nothing to it, Richie.

After lunch, a cheap one, my partner Mike took Richie along to a photographer's studio. We were doing a fashion shot and Mike tells me that it was on the glamorous side. I bet Richie loved that. Actually, Richie likes everything about my business except the smell. I know because he keeps wrinkling his nose. Still, I hope he keeps coming in. I'd like to expand his consciousness. He's too comfortable with his inbred and somewhat imbecilic prejudices. I know that advertising or any other kind of business is not his meat, but I'd like him to know the taste. He'll be a better teacher for it.

I'm willing to show him the whole thing in cutaway form. Maybe that's because down deep I'm a teacher, too. I think if he gave it a chance he'd be fascinated. Sometimes the action is speeded up like a Mack Sennett comedy. Right now it's more like a Warhol movie. If Richie has the patience, he will see the pace change and the mood lift. All business is manic. And we all ride the curves holding on for dear life, screaming, let me off, let me off. Then when it stops, we get back in line and pay our fifty cents for another ride on the roller coaster. So, just for the fun of it, I hope Richie hangs on. But I don't think he will.

Something else has come along. The riots. We can't help reacting, each in our way, to violence almost everywhere we look. It's happening in a dozen cities. Now. Tonight. Army tanks in the streets. While this is going on, Richie acts as though my interest in my work is an obscenity. For his part there is action to take. He's handing out leaflets around the Columbia campus. The message is that our government's unlawful action in Vietnam is responsible for the Negro violence.

The riots sadden me. Frighten me. Richie is glad. He's exhilarated. Yea, team!

Last night he told me that his is the politics of revolution. Revolution? Not, not violent revolution where people get killed, you understand. Just a speeding up of social reform. That kind of revolution. And in this respect the riots are good. Am I being dense? Reactionary? I don't think he knows what he's talking about. I think he's working for something he really doesn't want. He's using words that either he doesn't understand or I don't. What does he mean by revolution without violence? We have violence now. Does he really think that there is no one to fight back, that the other extreme has no guns, no anger, no cause? Or maybe he's not worried because he knows we won't let it get out of hand.

Who are we? The same we who have asked for, paid for, voted for, and are still working for what Richie says he wants. Yes, we're slow. But it's still to be proved that riots are faster. So far all that Richie has proved to me is that he disapproves of my old-fashioned liberal ideas, like integration.

Can it be? Can it be that Richie's generation invented sex, music, art, education, peace, understanding, dignity of man—all in the short few years since they first found hair around their privates? Is it possible that my generation has produced only frustration, war, prejudice, and greed? Can any educated kid, any kid really believe that? Or is it some kind of game and we're *it* as long as we accept their rules? Whatever it is, something is happening. It's happening fast. I'll give them that much. But that's all I'll give them on this particular kick. Richie can't tell me that Rap Brown is a better man than Martin Luther King. He can't tell me it's okay to kill your neighbors indiscriminately because you've been discriminated against. He can't tell me that the Germans didn't do the same thing to the world for much the same reason. He can't tell me that I live a lie and he lives the truth, that what I have done is nothing—not until he has done something.

Handing out leaflets is easy. What is hard is to make the system work. If Richie thinks he knows any way to make it work better, so people can live happier, longer, let him tinker with the system. But until he can show me a better one, any talk about throwing this system away makes me very nervous or, to use Richie's word, paranoid.

We said it all to each other a few nights ago and we weren't smiling. It was good for us to get it out. Somehow we moved closer to each other. He knows that I'm at a disadvantage in our arguments; that I know something stinks; that I, too, want to see movement; that I'm counting on his questioning, complaining, and pressure as much as he's counting on my patience, practicality, and responsibility.

The summer is thickening, and writing these pages is becoming more of a task. When the summer is over this book will be ended, whether I have finished it or not. There are many things that I feel compelled to talk about, but often I cannot connect them to experiences Ernie has shared. We have agreed to package only those moments relevant to the initial premise of the book; sometimes the most important things that happen are so quietly personal that I cannot make them accessible to Ernie. Consequently we have begun to lose each other's trail. He would like me to respond to certain aspects of his life with sincere enthusiasm, but I can only apologize for my disinterest.

My scheduled confrontation with "the business world" never really came off. I did linger about his office for a few days, but things were so slow that he himself found little to do. The business lunch which I have written about had for me a symbolic impact because it was contrived as material for this book, but it was relatively unimportant in itself. Ernie is continuing his efforts to precipitate some kind of activity in his office (for his own sake more than for mine) but the whole idea has become stale. I now have no taste for business; to be provoked to write about it I would at least require some distaste.

One day that I spent at Ernie's advertising office was eventful, but only in an experience outside the office. I went with the art director to a photographer's studio where a high-fashion model was being transferred to paper. I was fascinated to observe such a model in three dimensions; I had believed that these flash-tanned creatures could only exist on the two-dimensional surface of a magazine page. She was a slick chick. Click. . . .

I was intimidated by her monumental presence. She was probably over six feet tall, her facial bones created caverns where there ought to have been cheek, her lean legs were those of a young stallion, only longer; she had mini things to recommend her. All in all, she was a fine steed. I had always dreamed of being stomped on by such a girl. It was reassuring to know that my fantasy need no longer be confined to paper mannikins; such creatures do exist in the flesh, although it may be liquid rouge running through their veins.

The photographer, the studio, the model, all interested me in the same way as several scenes from Antonioni's film *Blow-Up*. I would probably have been less interested if I had not seen that film. The association of an actual experience with a cinematic creation glamorizes the basic experience; I was responding to the studio more as the source of a film than as a real studio. I do, however, admit that I fancied the whole thing, and going back to Ernie's office seemed like that much more of a drag.

At this point I feel no impulse to discuss business. Talking about a photographer's studio where some pictures were being shot for one of Ernie's ads is about as far as my inspiration will carry me. Ernie, I think, resents my unwillingness to immerse myself in the business world. He tells me that boredom and anticipation are very much part of that world. I accept what he says but I cannot muster the enthusiasm to wait out the calm. Ernie was eager to try pot; in a few hours he had a full experience and the afterglow of an initiate, but he did not have to extend his involvement over a period of days or weeks. I feel that he is construing my reluctance as a personal rejection of his daily life; the implications seem to be greater for him than those entailed in a mere backstepping on one experiment for the book. As I step back from business I suppose I'm stepping on Ernie's toes. I guess that's what this book is really about.

Ernie wanted me to face advertising as a "truly creative experience" where I would be instrumental in the conception and execution of at least one concrete piece of work. I am sure he felt that I would want to praise such an effort in which I had participated. Or he would want an honest declaration of defeat if I could not function in his world, failing in the work he handles quite well every day. Perhaps he would have wanted me to write just a detailed description and analysis of what it was like to be around his office. I am taking the trouble to state these possibilities because I know that Ernie wanted some kind of recognition and was concerned beyond the sake of the book with what I would write. Anything that goes into this book will, hopefully, reach many people; as a subversive counterforce anything I might say in praise of the advertising business (specifically my uncle's) would have the weight of an objective testimonial. Ernie doesn't need my testimonial as such, but I know he cares about what I say to the world. In the same way I was anxious for him to be sympathetic to marijuana; he was, and it was as if the authorities were condoning my illegal indulgences. It was as if for a few hours he made pot legal (maybe that's why in a way I resented his turning on—he destroyed an illicit thrill by his authoritative approval).

I'm afraid I will not be able to return Ernie's approval. I feel very slimy; I've managed to slip out of a tedious commitment to Ernie's office; there's little I can say approvingly or disapprovingly about it. Partly, I am lazy; I don't feel like working this summer. I am writing a book and taking a course at Columbia. It is a graduate course in art history dealing with Gothic art from the twelfth through fifteenth centuries. I would rather spend my days in those centuries, reading about them, than Ernie's office, even though his office is air-conditioned and the art history library is not. I have been reading approximately one book each day; I actually spend more time reading literature, and studies in comparative religion (one of my particular interests this summer) than I do in reading art history, but even the dullest art history book gives me a greater sense of freedom than being in an office. I don't like being confined; I want my time to be at my own disposal. I suppose I'm spoiled.

If I felt that being in an office was intrinsically more meaningful than being in a book I would attempt to restructure my life. But I can't see the virtues of business. I'd rather be free; you can always put down a book. In Ernie's language, I guess I'm "copping out" by staying away from his office. My generation is notorious for its cop-outs. I had agreed to sniff around business and tell of the smell in these pages, but my nose is stuffed; there was a draft in the library.

Last night Ernie and I had another political argument. It is hard to avoid them when the city and country are embroiled in racial riots and an escalating war in Vietnam. Ernie likes to think of himself as a progressive liberal. I suggested that his concept of progressiveness is in reality a kind of local humanism. He is directly concerned with the welfare of his employees, his friends, his immediate community, and other causes in proximity to himself; about these concerns he takes active measures, aiding generously with money and conviction. But on the national and international levels I think he loses perspective. Any possible progressiveness is crippled by conflicting personal interests; he usually reverts to the comfort of his own worldly philosophy as the substitute for a painful position. Of course he has every right to be indecisive about every issue, but certain attitudes which he has proclaimed have been, in my eyes, anything but progressive. Actually, I think *progressive* was originally Ernie's word. I don't see how anyone can be progressive without understanding the roots of the issue they're being progressive about. For that reason I prefer to be radical first and "progressive" later. Ernie is neither, so I guess he is what one may call a "liberal."

Whenever we argue about politics we inevitably polarize our own positions. This summer I think I have become more militantly radical than all during the past year, when I went to SDS meetings every week. Of course it's not only talking to Ernie that drives me to such extremes; this summer I have the time to observe carefully how this country is falling apart. Ernie always seems to come out of our arguments sounding like a staunch conservative. It's actually pretty funny because if anything, he is certainly not that. I am so far to the left of his left that he seems relatively to the right. I do know, however, that after our debates he will sometimes speak to one of his friends who is still less to the left and Ernie will come out sounding like an anarchist or at least a lover of Mao. I have a sneaky suspicion that in those discourses Ernie might be appropriating some of my positions, the same ones he fervently attacks. The mechanism of debate can be peculiarly self-defeating.

This nation is cracking under the strain of a viciously stupid foreign policy and a fatly complacent domestic policy. The most hopeful sign I have seen in the past year has been the rioting in the black ghettos. The Negroes are now fully realizing that they must act if they are to win the rights they deserve. Black power is a theme that has stunned many white people who like to think of themselves as the benefactors of the black race. When I entered college I joined CORE; my conscience demanded that I participate in the movement. Now I have learned to mind my own business.

The cry for black power has taught me that people with convictions drawn from a sense of empathy are never trusted and most often resented by the people who are being directly victimized. I understand exactly how the blacks have been driven to violence after observing so many whites filling their souls with the vicarious thrill of a social crusade. White men ride at the head of the civil rights movement in big cars fueled by Negro gas-station attendants.

I have learned to fear and to respect the black people, which is more important than "helping" them. And I hope as they see me fighting my own battles they will come to respect me. Black power has put an end to the continuing yearly progression of fashionable crusades and deprived mechanical white crusaders of another chance for glorious victory or defeat (it really doesn't matter as long as it is glorious).

One year I joined in to "ban the bomb"; another year it was stylish to demand "civil rights"; this year the call is for "peace in Vietnam." But where is the real immediacy of any of these causes for me? It is difficult to act on an abstraction. It has taken the exclusiveness of black power for me to realize that my battle with society also must be concrete and personally direct; conviction can only be sincere when the battle is to improve your life and not your soul. As I see things now the only real issue for me at this time is draft resistance. I can meaningfully express my general outrage about the war in Vietnam by specifically resisting the immediate threat of being drafted to serve in that war. Protest without some personal investment, without putting something on the line, becomes hollow; it becomes no more than a caricature of itself. That's why some students, to protest the war in Vietnam, have illegally burned their draft cards and risked arrest; protest alone is legal and safe.

I see the Negro riots as an undisciplined but similar expression of such personal investment. Each black person is putting his life on the line to affirm his belief in the cause, and there has been enough death and destruction in those riots to make each individual aware of the risks. Although there seems to be much potentially constructive energy wastefully dissipated in those riots, the white man must realize that only in this way can the black community declare its unity and independence as a whole from the white community; the riots are a kind of perverse celebration of the new faith that the black community has in itself. Just like fireworks, riots have a mass appeal and drain the complacency of many previously uncommitted Negroes.

I am not a lover of violence—I would not want to be caught dead in one of those riots—but it is clear to me that the model for such violence is the aggressive policy of our government itself. These riots are the way we, in this country, have come to know the anguish and ruin we have inflicted on Vietnam. It seems to me that apart from their terrifying social impact, more symbolically, these riots are serving to shove the government's foreign policies down the government's domestic throat. And I think this government is choking.

One evening a neighbor of my uncle's dropped by the apartment to borrow a cup of Scotch. At the same time we were working on the manuscript, and he rudely insisted on finding out what we were writing. He was a stockbroker, a man terribly aware of the influence of national and international affairs on the life of the market. Part of his job, he believed, was to keep himself diligently well-informed—but he could not distinguish the number of his facts from the worth of his facts. He talked like a ticker-tape machine and I felt like telling him to go look for a parade.

Ernie silently brought out the Scotch and offered the man the entire half-filled bottle in an effort to get rid of him as quickly as possible. This stockbroker, however, insisted on taking only a cup, and then began to drink it in the apartment. A conversation became unavoidable.

Of course he was very interested to hear about our book, especially anything that had to do with my radically anti-Establishment politics. Without allowing me to go beyond the few succinct aphorisms I used at first to sketch my political views, he blasted me with facts and figures from his arsenal of statistics. But his politics were only politics. He was so obviously trying to corner me that I felt like saying to him that the only way he could understand my most basic political attitudes would be by asking me questions that had nothing to do with politics. Since he was too vain to realize that for himself, I wasn't going to take the trouble to enlighten him.

Soon after our conversation began I thought the man was painfully boring but I resisted such a hasty conclusion for fear that I may have been defensively rationalizing a truly impressive political assault. But as his harangue gained in tedium I understood that he was not merely boring but cursed with a pervasive lack of imagination.

We were arguing about Vietnam; his position supported administration policy and favored continued military escalation. I realized, however, that our divergence of thought over any particular issue was inconsequential. What was critical were our totally different categories of thought. The "political reality" of the world situation which he accepted as absolute and empirically evident I challenged as being merely his subjective interpretation of the minute amount of political "hard data" that does exist. He could not, however, accept even in the most limited sense that I might have been thinking of the world situation in completely different categories from his and that when we used the same terms they might have had a substantially different meaning for me than they did for him.

"Realism" versus "Idealism" was not the crux of our disagreement. Every situation seems to project its own internal logic according to the perception of that situation by any given individual. But because he had mastered the logic of a political situation as he saw it, he vainly assumed that he had exposed "reality." In foolishly attempting to communicate with this man I was forced to deal with issues in the categories of his choice; and logically, my logic seemed faultier than his. In desperation I suggested that he was not making a fair attempt to conceive of any political approach to life that could be angularly opposed to his own and yet still be valid; and he was not allowing for the possibility of an approach to life that was not political but could still be politically effective. He had no intuitive concept of peace; he thought of it only as an interim between wars.

When I presented these remarks he staunchly refused to acknowledge them as being at all relevant to our discussion. At that point I made some feeble excuse and left the room. I had to get away from that man. There was no point in continuing an argument with one who refused to believe that he didn't know what he didn't know. For much the same reason that I was forced to leave the room, many of my younger contemporaries have been forced to leave home.

What I found in common between my uncle and his unwelcome visitor was an arrogance about the accuracy of their perception and the infallibility of their understanding of experience. Although this arrogance has, I think, been modified in Ernie (perhaps because of his involvement with me and my generation) there seems to be an intense conceit among middle-aged people about the very fact that they have had more experience than the so-called younger generation. Without a thought for the variety and quality of experience (refusing to consider the differences between their experiences and their children's), they can think only in terms of the quantity of experience and demand respect for the authority of age with no reasons given. Does the oldest person always have to be the wisest person?

As you might have guessed, I'm still on my first
marriage, eighteen years, and it looks as though it
will go on forever. I think my wife is beautiful, except
when she's angry. My children are beautiful, too, except when they're greedy. I'm beautiful, too, except
when I'm hungry. That's all you really have to know
about my family, except that they are presently living
in our almost-finished new house on Fire Island. If you
want to know more, come and visit us, but call first.

For Richie and me Fire Island is the neutral zone. It
is my Tara. And Richie doesn't feel guilty about the
richness of the upper-middle-class life there. Something
about the look of the Island, the politics and the bare
feet and the mix of people, all of whom love the place,
is very sweet and comforting. My wife and children are
happy there. I'm happy that they're happy. They're
happy that I'm happy that they're happy. I share a
sailboat with a close friend and neighbor. I play a bad
game of tennis with sociable partners. I go to dumb
parties and drink too much. I feel handsome and
strong in my bare feet and white pants and open-collar
shirt that shows the tan. I involve myself in the politics
and do things to help overprivileged people and their
kids keep from flipping because of overprivileged boredom. I belong. My family belongs. My friends belong.
It's been that way for more than ten years. And the security is terrific. Anybody who doesn't like it doesn't
know what they're missing.

Ernie would like me to talk about Fire Island within

the context of our friendship, but the Fire Island scene in essence displaces our friendship; to my mind at Fire Island Ernie rigidly resumes his identity as my uncle —that is, as husband of my aunt and father of my cousins. In that I am relating to my aunt and cousins as well as to Ernie, he becomes part of a structured pattern of family life.

The privacy of our relationship as two equals with respect to this book is obscured at Fire Island by the privacy of his relationship to his wife and children. Inevitably, his attitude toward me conforms to the way his children and wife see me, as cousin and nephew. Although human relations are not as rigidly structured as a diagrammatic analysis would make them seem, it is precisely those structured elements of Ernie's family life at Fire Island that have allowed me to enjoy myself there for so many years. When I am there, I am free. Any friendship is a kind of obligation, but when I can think of Ernie as my uncle, I can temporarily forget about my commitment to him as a friend. I merely fulfill my role as nephew and cousin and go my own way. I have other friends on Fire Island, and others to make; those others are girls.

Ernie is neutralized by his family. I can move in and out of the family scene at will, without being constrained as, at times, Ernie is. I look forward to being with his children; his nine-year-old daughter is a sparkler of giggles and grins which charge my delight when I see her; his thirteen-year-old son is more contemplative and I am beginning to be able to communicate with him in a mature way. Ernie's wife and I are in many ways kindred spirits. She grew up in Greenwich Village and went to the same high school I attended; in fact she was the person who suggested the possibility of my going to the High School of Music and Art, which unquestionably redirected my whole life. I am unequivocally fond of Judy, but I know I could never be her husband and sometimes thinking about Ernie's compatibility with her makes me realize things about Ernie's nature that I could never guess from knowing him alone. Of course they're not always so compatible. More than anything else at Fire Island I enjoy my status and immunity as Ernie's nephew; when family responsibility becomes burdensome, as it can in the self-indulgent environment of Fire Island, I do not doubt that Ernie envies my more detached affiliation with his family. Can it be that he wishes he were his own nephew?

My position at Fire Island affords me all of the comforts of an affluent family and all of the conveniences of an independent existence. I can cut out from the tedium of family life at will and yet return to the security of an open home. Going out to the Island whenever I choose on weekends allows me a kind of hit-and-run vacation spread out in bursts over the whole summer; I can think of no better arrangement. Considering my often conflicting social involvements, a hit-and-run curriculum is ideal.

Those intimacies, however, are outside the scope of my relationship this summer with Ernie. Let it suffice to say that I have always had a place in my heart for Fire Island; when I was fifteen I disposed of my virginity in a babysitter in my uncle's bedroom.

Since he was fifteen I've envied Richie, having a place like Fire Island to come to at his age. I'm sure he's always made out like mad with all our different mothers' helpers and they with him. Fair exchange. He and my kids dig each other very much. There's a lot of laughing when he's around. My wife dotes on him. My friends are friendly and warm toward him. He's always running into people he knows from the city. Why wouldn't Richie be happy there? Why wouldn't anybody be happy there? The beach stretches thirty miles along the ocean and a few blocks north there is the great South Bay. We now live in a little community called Corneille Estates, but we used to own a house a few blocks away in Fire Island's big city of five hundred homes and a dozen stores, restaurants and bars, Ocean Beach.

It is not inexpensive there. The merchants, bless their trusting souls, invite everyone to charge everything. Even the little kids have charge accounts. The homes cost a lot more than they're worth anywhere else in the world and the bank gives you a lot less of a mortgage. The society, far from the swinging jet set, is very family-oriented. They are sophisticated, however, being mostly New York City apartment dwellers and they make their very good livings in all the high-paying professions you can think of. Most of them didn't have it ten years ago. Me neither.

There are fishing and sailing and tennis, and a camp for the kids and a club for teen-agers, and cocktail parties and dinner parties and after-dinner parties and after-party parties. And everyone is content, except those who are discontent, and bored and lonesome and jealous and insecure and frustrated and just plain sick. Of course I don't know any of those people, I've just heard about them. But it makes you wonder. If you can't be happy on Fire Island, where in the hell can you be happy? The men seem mostly okay; it's the women who need a vacation away from their vacation homes. It seems kind of crazy. A guy works all year for a little time off at a gorgeous place he hardly gets to use, and can hardly afford, then it turns out that his wife just has to get away. He should take her to Newark.

The kids on Fire Island are pretty nice, except they get everything they want and they hardly see their parents, who wonder if maybe the children shouldn't be in a camp in the first place, because after all Fire Island is so free and a child can so easily get into trouble.

Most of us suffer in varying degrees from these problems, and the biggest problem of all is the guilt that comes with knowing that you're ungrateful. The people who seem to enjoy Fire Island the most are those who can afford it least. That's to say younger, less involved couples. They're in heaven. And, honestly, that's the way I feel most of the time when I'm there, except when I see my own family threatened by the Rich Bitch Syndrome. And then I do something about it. I yell my goddamn head off. But not last weekend.

Almost as soon as Richie and I were in the car headed that way, our feelings about each other came back to where they had been before we started this book. Once again I was the good old uncle, the family man, the provider of steaks, beer, sunshine, sailboats, mothers' helpers and a vacation house full of goodies. Once again I was unchallenged. I was the big man again and Richie was the delightful young fella, with the good future, my smart nephew. I drove the car because I can drive better. I know the way. Before we took the ferry I called my wife from Bay Shore and she met us at the ferry dock with raincoats. It had been a wet trip. We walked past our old home, which was now rented, and we were properly nostalgic. Then the tall, new house, with lights alive in every window, greeted us and it was beautiful in the dusk and the rain. I saw it reflected in Richie's enthusiasm and I knew how I had missed that enthusiasm these last weeks. But here it was again.

Then came my kids and the kisses and the jokes and a drink, two drinks, and a big family supper and everyone in a good mood in the new house with all the new furniture and the tall, tall old-brick fireplace and the view of the ocean and the Bay and Richie telling us how wonderful it was (we were). It was like *McCall's* magazine. It was also great to have Richie home with us again.

I had thought that a few of my close friends who knew about the book would be inclined to talk to Richie about it. I mentioned this to him and he said he hoped I wouldn't mind if he cooled it. He didn't have to; my friends cooled it first. That was a little surprise.

Actually, Richie wasn't too available. He spent a good part of the weekend perched like a bird on the little upper deck that adjoins our bedroom. It's the highest spot in the house, still unfinished without guard rails, and this suited Richie fine. He even convinced my wife, who is on the cautious side, and my kids, who aren't yet allowed out there, to join him. I saw them all sitting up there waving to me as I came up the wooden walk from a trip to Ocean Beach. I stopped at the refrigerator, grabbed a few cans of beer and joined them. It was very nice.

He also hung around our pretty mothers' helper a lot, "trying to make her feel like a member of the family," he said. I'm not sure which family he had in mind. But she seemed glad for his company.

I lost track of him Saturday night. But apparently he was doing fine at the Sea Turtle, a local pub that caters to my set for food and Richie's group for frug, or whatever they're doing these days. He said he had never danced better. On Sunday we went sailing together.

"Okay to invite a girl I know?" Richie asked.

"Sure! I like girls."

She got seasick and we had to put her ashore with much apology on her part.

"She hasn't been feeling well lately," Richie told me. "She expects her boyfriend home from Europe next week."

"So what has that got to do with her wanting to throw up?"

"Well," he said factually, "she's probably gone back on the birth-control pills."

"Oh," I said. What else was there to say? I wondered whether Richie knew or surmised. But I didn't ask him how he might have come by such personal information.

I had another little surprise Monday morning when we left the Island. I was on my way to meet the marketing executive of a company we work for. We were to leave for Chicago at eight o'clock from Kennedy Airport. He had picked the hour, not me. Richie would drop me off, then drive the car back to the city. In order to make it we had to get up at 5:30 A.M. I woke up feeling as though I had just gone on birth-control pills, too, but I really didn't know that I was sick yet. I never can tell how I feel at 5:30 A.M. When we got to the ferry dock, it turned out we were thirty minutes too early because the boat we had in mind hadn't been scheduled for a year.

When we got to the parking lot on the mainland, our car battery was dead. The parking lights we had used to drive in the rain on the previous Friday evening had been left on. Richie felt awful because he had offered to park the car so I wouldn't get wet. Now I had a real problem, but the parking attendant solved it by calling a nearby garage. They jumped the battery and five minutes later the car was running. By this time I was feeling quite shaky, but still not sure if it was a virus, the hour, or the aggravation. Now it was going to be tight. We stopped at the nearest phone booth to make sure there would be a message for my client when he arrived at the airline counter.

When I left the booth I said to Richie, "Okay, let's go home."

"You mean Kennedy?"

"No, I mean home to New York City. There are too many things telling me not to fly today, including my belly."

"What about your client?" he asked.

I said I had left word that I was sick and wouldn't be coming.

"Will he go on without you?"

"I don't know. I think so. He has distributors to see. I was just going along to tell the advertising story. I don't think he'll miss me too much."

The surprising thing was Richie's reaction. He was really impressed with me. Apparently I had done a very cool thing. But I'm always very cool before I throw up. Still, I suddenly seemed not to be a sell-out in having obeyed all the mystical signs, to say nothing of my stomach, instead of acting "gung-ho," "the show must go on," as Richie must have expected. In having done as any other reasonable man would have in my circumstances, I think, it must have appeared to Richie that I had flaunted authority and conformity, and I must say I enjoyed being a hero, even a nauseous one.

When I got home I crawled into bed and slept for a few hours. I awakened feeling a lot better and I thought I might go into the office for the rest of the day, but I didn't. Instead, I took a walk around the neighborhood, got a haircut, grabbed a sandwich at the local luncheonette, came home, and spent the afternoon in my air-conditioned bedroom working on this book.

I must say that really knocked Richie out. "Be sure you put it in the book," he told me. So now it's in the book. What do you make of it?

All in all, this seemed to be my day to understand and to be understood. When Richie called at about seven, he first asked me if I had gone to the office.

"No."

Then he asked if I would like to join him and some of his friends for dinner.

"Sure."

They were waiting in front of the Orange Julius at 110th Street and Broadway. Pale-bearded Willard, whom I had met before, and another Christly looking boy named Simon, and clean-shaven Richie, whom I suspect of not being able to grow a beard. They held court on the corner for about ten minutes, seeming to know and have something vital to impart to almost every kid who came by. It was like the opening scene in *Guys and Dolls*. Any second I expected a chorus of "I've Got the Horse Right Here."

Simon had just spent a student year in India. So there was some talk about going to an Indian restaurant. They asked me what I preferred. I said I didn't care. I had the distinct impression that we were going to eat Indian food, but we ended up at a Hungarian restaurant a few blocks away. I followed them all the way to the back of the place and down and around to the front again until they found a table to their liking. There was some business with a charming little lady of a waitress who had been in the country only two weeks and didn't speak English; she just kept smiling as the boys made the order as complicated as possible. When things settled down a little, Simon, who had gotten the message about me, made a half-hearted effort to kid me about the advertising business. I grinned at his question and he laughed at my answer, and that was that. Willard had been the one in the West End Bar who had asked all those "When did you stop beating your wife?" kind of questions. All he wanted to know was if I had put him in the book and if I had quoted him correctly. If I had made him sound dumb, he said he was going to write a rebuttal. I assured him that I didn't have to make him sound dumb. And he thought that was pretty funny. Richie seemed to be enjoying my easy acceptance of and by his friends. Everybody was in a fine mood. As quickly as they got off me they were all over Simon with questions about his year in India. He never really had a chance to answer because they just kept asking and interrupting one another and laughing.

"You ever chew khat?"

"Khat?"

"You know, it makes your mouth all red and gets you high."

"Oh yeah. Only it's called pung and doesn't make you high. It's like a mild stimulant."

"They smoke much pot in India?"

"Oh no, Brahmins don't smoke. But they mix a kind of hash into the candy and everybody gets high for dessert."

"Hey, candy. Wow! Great!"

"And it costs about three cents apiece."

"Wow!"

I couldn't really follow it all. For example, he might have very well said pong or ping instead of *pung* and I wouldn't have known the difference. I think they were having the same problem, only nobody cared. The meal went fast. And around the time for dessert they were involved in Indian music. Willard had some Indian records we had to hear. So we went to his apartment nearby. It was in a respectable-looking elevator building. The apartment itself was not so respectable-looking. He shared it with several other students and they each had their own what, for the want of a better name, you might call studio bedroom, all in various artistic states of disarray. Williard's room was a masterpiece. It was like one big ashtray. There were no other ashtrays in the room. Near the bed on which I sat was a glass-topped table covered with butts, and two other small items: a very smart stainless steel clock that unaccountably showed correct time, and a little postage scale. "Just what every home needs," I remarked. "A postage scale."

"Willard is always afraid of being cheated when he buys pot. He likes to make sure he's getting his money's worth—which in any case is impossible," Richie told me.

"What do you do, Willard, when you find out you've been cheated?" I asked. He shrugged and said, "Do you have a cigarette?"

All evening Willard had been carrying a comic book which he was very anxious for Simon to peruse. It appears a new character had joined "The Hulk" and "Thor" and some of the other superheroes. It was "The Silver Surfer." Richie said that he wanted me to see some of the books so he could show me the cinematic techniques in the drawings that had made these things so "in."

"Here," said Willard, and he heaved an armload of superhero comic books that he had taken from somewhere, from whence I know not, but now they were scattered all over the bed and floor.

Willard is to be married in about a month and I asked Richie where he and his wife would be living.

"In Willard's apartment," Richie told me.

I said "So I guess things will be a little neater." I guessed wrong. Richie explained that they were living together now and half the junk was hers, including most of the comic books. Apparently it's a marriage made in heaven. I can't help smiling as I think of the first time they entertain their in-laws.

The fact is, the more I get to know these kids, the more I find to smile about. Ten years from now they'll be well on their way toward running the world. Ho! ho! ho! Please don't console yourselves with the thought that they will change overnight. I think everything else will change a little first. Although I think even Richie would admit that Willard's room, with the trash strewn around as though it were seed sown by a farmer, was just a bit overstated. But everything is overstated for them now, especially the music and the pot, which came on and came out almost as soon as we were settled in. The music coming from the twin speakers—which, along with the turntable and amplifier, appeared to be the only thing in the room that had ever been cleaned—was not Ravi Shankar, but Brahms.

As for the pot, Willard offered it with the same hostlike efficiency with which I serve drinks to my guests. It came in a corncob pipe that was passed around like a peace pipe. Could the American Indians have smoked pot in their peace pipes? Maybe so, maybe that's how they made their peace. I'll have to ask a hippie about that someday. Of course he'll tell me it's so, even if it isn't, but I'd like to hear it. As they passed the pipe back and forth with much relighting because the grass was slightly damp and burning badly, they offered me my turn. I had not intended to smoke pot again in this book, or perhaps ever again. In any event, I wanted to think about it. Still, I did not refuse the pipe. Would Randolph Scott have refused to smoke with his Indians? Of course not. What's more, he would not have gotten high. And neither did I. Unlike my first experience, I could not turn on. Richie tells me it's because I really didn't want to and I suppose I must agree with him.

The boys felt it, however. Their reaction to the

music and to each other was beautiful. They simply had fun. I did too, just watching and listening. Brahms gave way to the Beatles and then to strange Indian music. In the foreground Willard and Simon sat on the floor, engaging in an impossibly funny improvisation which started with one misunderstood word. As I watched, I couldn't help feeling as I do when I watch my children playing; very tender, very sad that so soon they will find it so hard to play. Richie and I sitting on the bed participated very little. We just sat there watching two average, normal American superintellects playing at their games.

My class was over at 8 P.M. and I walked down to 110th Street on Broadway, where I had arranged to meet my friend Willard. In a couple of minutes he arrived and we walked down another block to my favorite little Cuban restaurant. At the Ideal Restaurant (as it is named) we had our usual dinner, although tonight we varied our selection somewhat; we had peppered steak with fried banana rather than with rice and beans. Our meal ended, as always, with a cup of espresso. This to my knowledge is the only place in New York where you can get a cup of espresso for a dime.

Willard and I contentedly removed ourselves from the restaurant and walked a few more blocks downtown. He was trying to convince me to go with him to see a Swedish film at a nearby theater; I was trying to convince him to stop convincing me. I knew I had to get some writing done; I couldn't bear having to tell Ernie again that I had finished no new pages. Each time he questions me I feel it is a threat; I must squirm and finally admit to having written nothing. At those moments I experience most vividly Ernie's role as uncle and as older adult; I resent his authority; I consider it merely the emblem of age, and I resent his dominion over me as his nephew. It is evident how tenuous friendship must remain when it can be displaced so abruptly by the authority of blood.

My contest of will with Willard about the Swedish film was suddenly discontinued. We came across an open storefront wherein we observed a boy and girl sandpapering the crudely replastered walls of the old store. They were both friends of Willard's. To minimize description and quickly characterize them, let me say that they were hippies; he wore a necklace and seemed to be fairly high, while she would have been less definitely characterized but for her unsaddled breasts and black tunic. By coincidence they just happened to be living together in my old building on 125th Street. As we found out, they were in the process of opening a jewelry shop and bead store. Whatever money they made would be put into a fund which would be used to purchase a communal farm with some others of their friends and business associates. They were also at the time looking for a ten-room apartment (for twelve people) they could use as their communal dwelling. Willard and I were in strong sympathy with their utopian program, so we helped them sand the walls. As we began to work they stopped. Willard and I drifted into a conversation about the work and play elements in our contemporary culture; our conversation became more animated as we became bored with the sanding. Willard's two friends were drinking orange juice, kissing and touching each other, as they stood together in a corner of the store—in front of the large dusty window. We decided that when play becomes compulsive, it becomes work. We had started sanding as play but stopped sanding as our playful discussion distracted us from what had begun to become work.

As I see it, all work becomes play either when you are stoned or living in a utopian socialist state. The two in the corner were trying to achieve both conditions and I think they were succeeding. The moment we began walking out of the door they calmly disengaged their embrace and resumed their sandpaper toil; it was as if it didn't matter to them whether they were kissing or scraping. When you are high, anything is at least as good as anything else, although some things are better. I imagine they would have preferred to prolong their embrace.

After leaving I regretted that Ernie had not joined us at the store. He would have thought of it as a "sand-in." Lately he has been very anxious to meet a few bona-fide hippies (if such a thing exists, which I doubt). I feel inadequate because I cannot readily fulfill this request. Although my hair right now is about as long as Byron's, Ernie knows I am not an occupational hippie. If anything, I might be a "closet-hippie," keeping beads and bells in my wardrobe to sort of cheer up the darkness. Actually all this is nonsense; I am a student, a lover, a writer, a friend, a son, a political activist, and an apprentice intellectual, and in that I manifest all of these discreet identities I cannot possibly be a hippie. "Hippie" is a consummate nonidentity, the embodied absence of all standard identities. In the idiom of mathematics a hippie would be a member of the "null set." And besides, the only bell I've ever owned has been in my alarm clock.

But I am not condescending. I respect the hippies. They have chosen their way of life by denying other alternatives. I sometimes feel very guilty about not being one of them; their life seems to be an alternative to choosing alternatives, an experimental and enviable position.

Ernie wants to meet some of these people. Meeting them, however, seems superficial to me. You must become a hippie to understand their way of life. Everyone acts like a hippie at some time or another even if it is just for a second, like when one walks out of an apartment when the telephone is ringing because one doesn't like the sound of that particular bell. It is merely a question of knowing when the hippie in you strikes.

For several years I've been aware of the schizoid aspect of the life I lead, as so many of us over forty do. It would be so easy to care about nothing or just one thing. For me it would be easy to care only for my work; to weave all the threads of family life and social life into the fabric of professional accomplishment; or to excuse all the waves I might make in the outer world as necessary to my inner world, caring only about my private life, wife, children, and community.

It would be easiest of all to care only about myself.

No such ideal of concentration is possible in the life I have created and which created me. My family, my business, my libido, and now my book keep me at war with myself. In order to function I have learned to establish a priority of interests and to curb my constant tendency to commit deeply to more people and ideas than I can handle. This doesn't really work very well. But it works better than my earlier efforts to convince myself and all the people who compete for my interest within my different lives that what is good for me is good for all of them. It isn't. It can't be. Unless someone is lying. But by the time most kids become old enough to achieve awareness, their parents have already begun to live by such lies.

The kids, who only want to care about themselves, feel threatened, compromised. They insulate themselves against the lie. They despise it and society which perpetuates it. They reject complicated commitments. They can't stand the sight or the sound of the older generation complacently working everything out, ignorant of or ignoring the little pieces of themselves that have gone to feed the lie of contemporary society. Still worse for the kids is any effort on the part of their parents to try to turn things around and actually live the overstated, oversimplified truth of young, total self-involvement. Most of all the kids resent us because we have not created a world where it is possible for them to go on as they are. They want peace, love, money, freedom, leisure, accomplishment, recognition, respect. Who's stopping them? Most of them will find their way, some will get lost, a few will even become hippies. Recently I have tried to meet some hippies, but all I've been able to find are some kids who use and reject the hippie culture. When Richie and I were first outlining this book I thought maybe we both could live in a hippie commune for a while. Of course I thought that Richie could arrange it, but he told me that he really had no connections in the hippie world. In fact, a title I had suggested for the book, *My Nephew the Hippie, My Uncle the Square,* bothered him mostly for that reason, and because it sounded too slick. I argued that it was typical of the overstatement and misunderstanding that pervaded both generations' ideas about one another. "Yes, but I'm definitely not a hippie," Richie answered. He didn't add that I wasn't a square, either. That, too, is typical. Kids are very precise when defining themselves but quite willing to generalize about us.

Of course, the tremendous volume of national magazine coverage recently accorded the hippie movement has made our involvement in this area somewhat less significant. Even what we believed to be slightly sensational revelations about pot in the beginning of our book have become just a footnote to stories in *Newsweek, Time, Life,* and *Look.*

What is significant to me is the disdain with which most kids I've met regard the hippies and their philosophy. While it's clear to me that action politics and pot promise to be with us from now on, hippie-love and LSD appear to be on their way out. I've discovered to my surprise that both my nephew and I suffer from acid indigestion.

I am afraid that I have become rather bored with the hippie-psychedelic culture that has flowered in the past few years. LSD has been the fertilizer. Its magical powers seem to have made it the twentieth-century philosopher's stone, the modern alchemist's panacea. Acid transformed the suffering beatnik into the beatific hippie. Acid can soothe a psychic sore while producing dream-filled blisters on the brain. Four years ago I took a twelve-hour LSD trip; it was one of the most fantastic and resounding experiences of my life. One must make a conscious effort not to become a "hippie" after tripping, or else become one by default. I made my decision; although I marveled at the LSD cosmos, my first excursion was my last.

Not everyone should take LSD, and yet some people should be compelled to take it. The major problem is the impossibility of knowing who should and who should not. Unfortunately, hallucinogens have been overexposed and commercially popularized. Any possibility of meaningful personal evaluation has been obliterated by the cultic propaganda and mythic incantations in blind praise of acid. The psychedelic movement must be decentralized and depublicized if the critical judgment of the individual is to become the determining factor in the decision whether or not to experiment.

The great danger of acid lies not in the psychocosmic experience itself but in the cultic seductiveness of the experience. Acid should not be taken as a required initiatory rite; instead it must entail an individual decision and an individual commitment. As long as LSD and other drugs remain misunderstood, condemned and illegal, the hippie-psychedelic subculture will flourish and the significance of the experience for the individual will continue to be eclipsed by the propaganda of the cult. Cults become fads and fads become obsolete. I believe that hippies are already becoming an anachronism and by the time this book is published we should be entering what I would call a post-psychedelic phase. Perhaps when LSD is forgotten I and others will try it again. As things are now, the expansion of consciousness is accompanied by a contraction of social tolerance. Only when a person can take acid without becoming one of the hippies, without being associated with their philosophy, without being channeled into a marginal culture will the use of hallucinogens be redeemed.

I discussed the East Village scene with my friend Willard as we continued walking down toward my apartment after leaving the bead store. We were both very curious about the hippie community on the Lower East Side. There seemed to be no need for us to move into their world, since many things (such as the new bead store) indicated that they were extending uptown into our world at Columbia. But we were not content to wait. Although we had been typically intellectual in our acid skepticism of hippies, my friend and I decided that we would have to dispense with this attitude and insinuate ourselves into their nonintellectual domain if we were to learn anything about that domain. This would also be a good chance of bringing Ernie into an even more extreme environment than the one he's been exposed to through me. At about the time of our decision to infiltrate this esoteric region of lower Manhattan, my stomach was beginning to acknowledge the obtrusive presence of very peppered steak. I left Willard and returned to the apartment where I told Ernie of my evening and repented my Spanish dinner.

The evening of our visit to the East Village, I was driven home by a business friend, a public relations man with whom we work. He had to meet someone later downtown and was killing time after a late meeting at my office. I had just fixed him a drink when Richie came in with his friend Willard.

The boys had a friend living in the Village who "knew the scene" and we were to meet him about nine. My public relations friend offered to give us a lift, but Richie and Willard seemed in no hurry. The talk was strained. Somehow I identified with Richie and Willard and realized that my colleague was saying all the wrong things. The boys were polite but uncommunicative, as our guest, a gregarious and charming man, tried to make talk about safe things, like the neighborhood, the weather. They didn't even bother to bug him about the public relations business.

We hadn't eaten; Richie and Willard, having refused a hard drink, were munching potato chips and drinking Coke from the can. My friend had to leave and again offered us a lift, if we would hurry. It was beginning to get too important and I could almost feel Richie's and Willard's reaction to his polite pressure. Now I was one of them and I wanted to say "We don't want to go yet." But instead I mumbled something about not leaving until all the potato chips were gone. "You know how it is with these hungry kids. Ha! ha! Speak to you tomorrow." He left—somewhat puzzled, I'm sure.

But isn't that the natural reaction to almost any encounter with the new generation? The frightening thing is that I understood. Somehow I understood that they wanted to go "high" to the East Village.

I wasn't at all surprised when Richie said, "Willard and I want to share a joint. Is that all right with you?"

"Sure."

"You don't want to smoke, do you?" Richie told me, knowing I didn't. Getting the answer he expected, he added "I think that's right, you should do it your way."

Ernie was waiting at the apartment when I arrived there with my friend Willard. I was surprised to find Ernie not alone, but with another middle-aged man. As it turned out, this was the fellow Ernie had hired to do some publicity work for his agency; business had been slow and Ernie felt it was necessary to get someone outside the agency to advertise his advertising. The public relations man had given Ernie a lift uptown from the office since we had arranged to meet at the apartment before venturing into the lower depths of the East Village.

The term *hippie* has meaning outside the hippie's own community only as a comparative concept. Compared to the p.r. man, Ernie seemed like the hippest thing Madison Avenue had ever expelled. Later Ernie remarked that he considered this other gentleman to be a "swinger" (after all, he would hardly allow the public image of his cool little agency to be distorted by a non-swinging public relations man). I didn't press Ernie on what he meant by a swinger; I find the whole idea very amusing and I've been around Ernie long enough to be familiar with the type of person denoted by that title. Before this summer began and before we traded terms in this book, Ernie used to think of himself as a swinger. By now I think the term has become for Ernie an embarrassing slip of the tongue, at least when he is with my friends. Although I refrained from questioning Ernie about the meaning of the word, my friend Willard did pursue it. It was like seeing Ernie slip on a planted banana peel as I listened to him formulate an instantaneous definition. I can't remember his specific explanation, but I do remember my critical impression; I thought of a swinger as an adult teeny-bopper in a society where the very expression had become awkwardly outmoded. I find it difficult to suppress the image of Benny Goodman chewing on his clarinet, swaying in a balloon-filled ballroom among a herd of admiring, dewy-eyed "swingers." This vision must, of course, be updated by replacing the balloons with psychedelic lights and electrifying Benny's clarinet; the "swingers" themselves, however, have never been updated and that is the mark of their absurdity.

While we were still at the apartment I could see Ernie delighting in a "cooler-than-thou" attitude toward the pleasant p.r. man. Part of the publicity for Ernie's agency was to be drawn from his involvement in writing this book and he was undoubtedly playing up the aloofness of his creative nobility. Ernie seemed to be forgetting that he is supposed to be "my uncle the square." But I did not forget to be his "nephew the hippie." I performed for the p.r. man with eccentric abandon. I put my bare feet all over the furniture, spoke in a garbled mumble, blinded myself by flicking my hair, and affected other mannerisms as they occurred to me. Reflecting on the whole scene I cannot help feeling that the p.r. man was so much a "swinger" that my hippie act went unnoticed. In the midst of my exotic performance he proceeded to tell me of a book he was currently attempting to publicize; it deals with the secrets of muscle-building and he seemed singularly impressed with it.

Ernie happily cooperated in the realization of my role as much as he worked at his own, but that may have been no more than his way of indicating his alignment with me in relation to the p.r. man. Willard put on a record as soon as we entered the apartment and I brusquely shuffled into the kitchen to put into service an unopened bag of potato chips. As I began munching, Ernie's friend mentioned that he would soon have to leave and that if we wanted a ride part of the way downtown we would soon have to join him. Ernie took his cue from my contorted silence and announced that it seemed as if Willard and I had not eaten dinner and that it was unthinkable to extract us from our depthy involvement with the potato chips and the music; any further animation would have to attend the demise of the potato chips and conclusion of the song. We agreed with no nod. The p.r. man made an ingenuous exit, after which I turned off the record and put away the sickening potato chips.

Ernie, Willard, and I amused ourselves for several minutes discussing the preceding several minutes. Willard and I decided to have a quick smoke, which canceled our hurry, and we postponed our immediate intention to leave. We were supposed to meet another friend of mine in the West Village at about nine o'clock, but as it turned out we were about an hour late. Willard wanted to read some parts of the manuscript Ernie and I were working on, and I proceeded to show it to him; he read it very quickly, but carefully, and seemed to enjoy what he read. His few brief critical comments launched Ernie into several voluminous explanations about various aspects of his life and business. Willard distracted him by asking new questions before Ernie could fulfill his own need to answer the previous ones, and all the while my mind was distantly seated among the iridescent sounds of another record I had just turned on.

Willard asked to see the manuscript and Richie brought it out along with the pot, which I thought was fitting. I've noticed that Richie has smoked a good deal more this summer than I thought he might after our earlier talks on the subject. I haven't said anything about it because I assume it has something to do with his comparatively light work schedule.

Willard was reading and flipping pages as you might flip through a magazine. At first I thought he was doing just that, flipping through. But every once in a while he commented or asked a question which showed complete comprehension. Richie reads like that too, as though he had taken a speed-reading course. But, after all, he's a professional student. He reads like Namath throws a football. Too bad he doesn't have Joe's trick knee to show his draft board.

The ninety or so typed pages and the joint were finished at about the same time. We had left off with the description of the evening at Willard's apartment. There was a detail I had not included that Willard told me was important. I had left it out because it had seemed ominous and out of character. During that evening Willard had been playing around with a cheap switchblade knife that he kept around as a paperweight or as some kind of perverse toy. He kept trying to flip it open and it wouldn't flip. He and Simon thought it was funny. I didn't. I was nervous and asked them to stop. I thought that at any moment it would fly open and out of Willard's hand and into Simon's chest, which was directly in front of the downward snap of Willard's arm.

Willard told me that it was my uncool, responsible attitude that prevented me from getting high and even brought them down a bit.

"Next time I'll let you kill each other," I thought of

saying. But I didn't mean it, and I didn't say it. Willard had been trying to tell me something and he meant it warmly and well. We are becoming good friends and he was just sorry that I had acted like a parent. I was sorry he had acted like a child.

After a while Richie called his friend on Christopher Street and we left. The boys modestly headed for the subway but I hailed a cab. To me it was just another cab ride but Richie, under the influence of the weed, kept exclaiming about the beauties of Seventh Avenue as we headed downtown through the light evening traffic. If pot can make Seventh Avenue and 26th Street beautiful, then it can't be all bad.

We finally left or we abruptly left; I can't be sure what it felt like but I do recall that Ernie said he'd "spring for a cab" down to the Village. There was a comic incongruity in extravagantly taking a taxi so that we'd have more time to spend among impoverished hippies. But apart from that I thought the taxi ride was a fantastic experience. I particularly enjoyed the sensation of sharp stops and the blur of colored neon streets as the taxi shattered the air; my face was at the open window. Willard continued to pepper Ernie with questions and occasionally looked out of the window.

We arrived at my friend David's modest apartment on Christopher Street, whereupon I introduced Ernie and admired the kitchen area painted in Day-Glo chartreuse. Ernie finally caught our spirit and noted the lovely blue and brown labels on variously scattered jars, as well as pointing out the chromatic priority of a certain yellow plastic cup perched above the stall shower (with the pinkish-violet curtain) next to the white kitchen sink. We were all pleased with his astute color perception. Gradually our interest shifted from colors to textures and Willard, in particular, delighted in rolling his eyes across a piece of checkered burlap pasted to the door of the refrigerator; he was awed by the stunning contrast of sleek white enamel and the hairy, knotted cloth.

For me, the dullest part of the evening was our march through the East Village. I kept saying things I saw were "beautiful," but that was partly because of my mood and partly because I could think of little else to say when I felt like saying something. I had already begun to neglect Ernie's presence; I was walking ahead of him while he continued answering Willard's questions, which seemed to slow his pace.

Our route to the hippie district was straight along Eighth Street, which is like the undetached umbilical cord and channel of touristic nourishment for the embryonic East Village. As the street quietly winds around the Cooper Union School of Art, at first it unobtrusively becomes St. Marks Place, but from there on the subtle transition from west to east becomes blatant and St. Marks Place fully reveals itself with all the psychedelic splendor of commercialized hippiness. Before Eighth Street dissolved into St. Marks I had a symbolic encounter with an old girlfriend practically in the entrance to Ernie's old apartment building (he had lived on Eighth Street for several years before moving uptown).

I saw the vaguely familiar face of a girl, thinner now and with shorter hair, but still recognizable. I grabbed her as she passed and we startled each other into a passionate embrace lasting several seconds. I was tickled to a squealing joy by this dramatic encounter. I knew Ernie would be enviously struck by the spontaneity of such youthful affection. I had thought the girl was still in Alexandria, for which she had departed some months earlier, and my surprise to find her in New York was genuine. She had returned to this country at the outbreak of the Arab-Israeli war. For some reason I realized that I had wanted somehow to jar Ernie and this meeting was the defining and fulfillment of that most abstract wish. Ernie had been wanting to explore the hippie world but I had continually postponed the adventure. I personally felt no intimacy with the hippie scene and I did not want to debase myself by becoming an East Village tourist. At least meeting an old girlfriend and kissing her intently in the middle of the street gave me some sort of identity within the context of the Village and demanded Ernie's envying recognition, if nothing else.

The unexpected encounter reordered the plan of the whole evening. The girl I knew was with a friend who seemed to attach herself to Ernie and undoubtedly Ernie was flattered by her company. He continued to lag behind as we all resumed walking but now he was talking with the girl. Soon we were in the heart of the East Village, Tompkins Park, the garden of hippies. Nothing was happening in the park and so our wandering continued until we arrived at the most lavishly elegant of all psychedelic accessory shops, the Psychedelicatessen. With the girl, I wound my way through the dreamy clutter inside the shop, gasping every now and then from the aromatic density of the burning incense. Everything was "beautiful"; after about fifteen minutes I became substantially bored. Ernie was so involved conversationally with the other girl that he barely deigned to enter the shop and once he did, he left almost immediately. I bought a handful of peppermint-stick candies which I had lovingly intended to distribute to all of my friends, but when I sought Ernie I realized he had gone off on his own with the girl. I was stunned by his boldness. From that point on my imagination flourished in its attempt to account for Ernie's absence. Ernie was now having his own adventure; whether or not it had anything to do with hippies, I assumed I would find out when I read about it.

I was looking forward to the outing with an unsophisticated expectation of adventure. Actually my experiences with Richie have been anything but adventurous. The adventure has been all in our heads. We have traveled the worn paths we know so well: a trian-

gle from midtown East Side Manhattan to Upper
Broadway to Fire Island; from work to family to
friends. Yet it has all seemed new and strangely exciting. The Village, too, should not have been new to me.
I had lived there for about fifteen years. Beards, ban-
gles, beads; boys and girls together; boys and boys together; all colors and combinations of peoples con-
forming in their individualism—I found it familiar.

As we walked down Eighth Street toward the east, I
found little else familiar. Now there were four of us,
Richie, Willard, David (a Columbia friend of theirs),
and me. I suppose it had been that way for years, but
now Eighth Street seemed honky-tonk, harsh. And
there were so many people, all searching so hard.
"Where is It? Where is It?"

"Where is what?"

"I don't know! It!"

It must be something, or else why are all these people here trying to find it?

We stopped off at a garish pizza place. I was hungry. I offered to buy some for my companions—they
refused. Willard had gone across the street to the record shop. When he came in he picked up my orange
drink from the counter and gulped half of it. Then he
reached for my slice of pizza and took a couple of
bites.

"Hey," Richie said, protective of me, "he hasn't
eaten anything tonight," forgetting that neither had he.

Willard said "Sorry," looking as though he really
was.

I handed him the rest of the slice and the cup. "Go
ahead." Then I ordered several more slices and drinks
and everybody continued to munch and make comments about the campy plastic adornments, such as the
five-foot plastic lighted ice cream cone which adver-
tised the custard in the rear.

One of the boys asked: "What will the archeologist
of the future think when he digs it up?"

We wandered out along the street and turned into
Macdougal Street. There in the shadows, grotesquely

garbed, slim figures leaned in the doorways, on each other and in every direction. The corner of Waverly Place contained a complement of police and fifty or sixty kids milling about as though there had been an accident. Nothing was happening except that the cops were chatting with a couple of kids, casual and friendly. Maybe that's something. We crossed over and wandered catty-cornered back through Washington Square Park heading generally east toward Eighth Street again. I saw the same shadowy shapes, only now they sat on benches, almost inanimate. Between Greene Street and Broadway, I stopped to look at the apartment house we had lived in a few years back. I turned just in time to see a little miniskirted figure hurl herself into Richie's arms. She was a girl Richie had known in high school. They stood and talked in the middle of the sidewalk as everyone stood quietly about, one of the boys leaning on the fender of a car at the curb.

"He's never short on girls, is he?" I muttered to Willard, cocking my head in Richie's direction.

It went on for a long time, a strange tableau. Finally there were some incoherent introductions. I heard the words *my uncle* and said hello to Jane and her pretty little friend who, too, had been mutely standing by.

Then, as with a flock of birds, at some unspoken signal we all moved off together in odd formation. On the next corner stood a monstrous new apartment building. We all stopped again. I patted the marble wall in front on the few steps leading up to the entrance plaza, and I told of the luncheonette which had stood on this corner and of the old couple who ran it. I ate there almost every morning during my last summer in this neighborhood. The old lady who served everything so nicely would tell me of how they were fighting to save their place, and of the real estate interests who were trying to evict them; of how she would never give in.

"Where are they now?" It was Ellen. She was the only one who had been listening.

"Probably under this," I said, patting the tomblike marble slab.

Almost at the same moment Jane ran up to me and put a red flower through the buttonhole of my open-collar shirt. The stem scratched my chest. Richie, Willard, and David each got a flower, too. While I had been speaking to the old lady under the marble slab, Jane had picked the flowers from the narrow garden which decorated the plaza front. Authority in the guise of an irate tenant appeared almost at the same moment. He was a gross-looking man in his mid-fifties.

"You shouldn't do that. Those aren't your flowers," he complained.

"Flowers belong to everyone," Jane assured him sweetly.

"I'm going to call the doorman if you do that again."

And there I stood, a forty-year-old delinquent, one of the stolen flowers blazing on my chest, secretly sympathizing with the frustrated man who was only trying to be a good citizen. He saw it as an act of vandalism. Jane saw it as an act of love. Me, I wish I hadn't seen it at all. But I said to Jane as we moved on, "If I'm not careful, I'm going to be just like that man when I grow up."

We wandered into the East Village. Ellen knew that Richie and I were writing a book together. I surmised something had been said during the conversation in front of 50 East Eighth Street where I used to live, and she was curious. We walked and talked together, Ellen acting as my guide. There was really nothing much to see except ugly tenements and a few clubs like the Electric Circus, all of which looked the same from the outside. Ellen wanted to know about our book and I was glad to tell her. She asked what work I did and I told her. She reacted as expected. It was a case of "You seem okay. How could you be doing such a terrible thing?" Not in so many words, but with an incredulous look and a "Really?" and a shake of her head as if in amazement. I let it go at that.

I asked about the smoke-in in Tompkins Park every Sunday. She verified what David had told me. They all sat around smoking pot in front of the police who pretended that nothing really was going on, except that the city doesn't want any riots this summer in the East Village.

On Avenue A everybody went into a headshop, a psychedelic store that caters to potheads and acidheads. The hippies have brought with them a large commercial following. The publicity has attracted many such funny little shops and weird clubs, rather like a carnival attracts pickpockets. This shop was very pretty, all purples, pinks, electric blues, and chartreuse in op patterns. Incense burned on an Oriental shrine. There was a case full of pot-making devices for sale. I couldn't stand the place. It may sound funny coming from me, but the shop was too commercial. Ellen and I walked out while the others lingered.

Before Ernie disappeared there was no longer anywhere in particular to go, and once our star tourist had wandered off on his own my friends and I had no personal interest in extending our Village visit. But I thought Ernie might have gone off for a short time and would expect to meet back at the nearby apartment of the girl who remained with us. I suggested that possibility to the group and the girl gladly invited us back to her pad. We were all speculating vigorously on what might be the implication of Ernie's absence. Although we felt that his appropriation of the other girl was a harmless gesture, we could not suppress our various versions of a seduction fantasy. My feelings were especially ambiguous. On the one hand I took a perverse delight in the thought of Ernie seducing a young college girl after eighteen years of domestic married life; on the other hand I was hoping his exploit would end in failure and humiliation. The bitterness of this latter thought, I suppose, reflects my subtle but thriving resentment of Ernie's intrusion once again into my most

exclusive domain. A sexual intrusion, the assertion of
his sexual prowess among my peers, would be the most
critical threat to the psychological economy of our relationship; this summer that economy has been in a
quivering balance and certainly could not sustain any
overtly sexual jolt.

As we approached the apartment, the street seemed
to pulse with my alternate anticipations of Ernie's
presence and absence. We turned a corner and there
was Ernie sitting childishly on a stoop in front of the
building; the girl was crouched, not too close, behind
him. Little was said as we brushed by them on our as-
cent up the stairs to the apartment. My relief at finding
him there was, however, clouded by his brusque reply
when I asked him to join us upstairs; he said that he
would prefer to remain sitting outside; the girl's
agreeing nod acknowledged her complicity and provoked in my mind new speculations and renewed fantasies.

Ellen and I waited on the corner for the others and
then when they didn't come we walked ahead to Jane's
building, even farther east on a side street. We reached
the building after passing a hippie commune, a building painted with psychedelic designs. A few sad characters sat on the stoop. When we reached the walkup
where Jane lived we sat on the stoop, too. The only
hippie who had spoken to me had been in front of the
subway station at Broadway and Eighth Street. He was
standing there making a bold visual statement in his
mod jacket and ornamental necklace. In contrast to his
strong appearance, accentuated by profuse mustache
and hair, the girl who cringed behind him was so indis-
tinct I could hardly see her.

"Have you got a few pennies?" he asked. "Man, we
have to eat." We all dug in and got up some change. It
depressed me to see a dream, even a dream I couldn't
believe in, turn into such a nightmare of despair. How
they must hate the world, their parents, themselves, to

commit suicide and call it love. It is the ultimate in rejection of everything our society is. It is teen-age rebellion followed to its illogical conclusion. The only thing
cooler is death. But Richie and his friends want to live,
no matter what. The hippies have sacrificed themselves
for Richie, and Richie has accepted their sacrifice as
his due. I was depressed with all I saw; Richie was en-
thusiastic. He takes no responsibility for what the hippie is. He just takes what he likes and leaves the rest
behind. As an intellectual, a scholar, he feels he has
the right.

Ellen, on the other hand, had dropped out of college. Her protest had carried her a bit too far and
coming back is slow and painful. She had no idea of
what she wants to do, living for now and deferring as
many decisions as possible. She and Jane are planning
to move into a better neighborhood and a more expensive apartment, which they will share. I was surprised
to hear Jane say, as we had been walking, "I want par-
quet floors." They can afford it, because they work as
waitresses in one of the clubs and earn $140 a week.
They usually work until 3 A.M., but this was a night off
and they had just been wandering around. Perhaps it's
symbolic that they were walking west toward Fifth
Avenue—which is still, as are many West Village side
streets, serenely beautiful. Where we were now sitting
was not so beautiful.

When Jane, Richie, Willard, and David arrived ten
minutes later we were invited upstairs. I was enjoying
the quiet intimacy of the stoop and the last thing I
wanted to see was another psychedelic apartment, nor
did I want to hear the Stones or watch the pot ritual
enacted again. So in my new-found freedom to please
myself I said: "I'd rather sit here for a while." Ellen
must have approved because she didn't say anything. I
didn't know what Richie and the others thought, but I
can imagine. I can also imagine what you're thinking.

Henry Miller would know what to do with a situation like this. However, I am not Henry Miller and I
must deprive you of your fantasies and tell the truth.

In this era of mass-media pornography truth is
stranger than fiction, and admittedly in this case duller.
I might say that as I sat alongside this miniskirted
twenty-one-year-old of neat figure and sweet face, no
erotic thought crossed my mind. It just stomped in
wearing heavy boots, tracking mud all over the place,
and hung around trying to look wise. But soon, with
both disappointment and relief, I permitted myself to
fall ungracefully back into the role of husband, father,
and middle-aged researcher for a book about youth.
Dignity, damn it, had again defeated desire. Cool again
had been displaced by talkative curiosity.

Leaving Ernie downstairs, we swallowed our fantasies and entered the apartment; it was a standard East
Village pad. The dominating odor was of cat urine
masked slightly by the fragrance of wet wool (a couple
of sweaters had been washed and were drying on the
living-room floor). Any further objective appraisal
could not be made since as soon as we entered it was
announced that this four-room apartment cost only
fifty-six dollars a month; instantly our esthetic doubts
dissolved as we praised such a virtuous bargain. Rents
are outrageously high in the Columbia area; besides,
any apartment can become a villa if there's enough
grass around.

Having just returned from the Mideast, my girlfriend had a fertile pantry. In a kitchen closet she revealed two or three different vintages of pot and an
impressive quantity of hashish, both the dark and light
varieties. Like any proper hostess she immediately
opened her pantry to our pleasure. She suggested a
cocktail (hashish mixed with marijuana) but my
friends were interested only in the superior intoxicant;
pot is common but hash is a treat to be savored by itself. As the tiny clay pipe was passed around I for-
feited my turn; I didn't feel like smoking again that
evening and I was somewhat distracted by my thoughts
about Ernie. Before we came upstairs he had added

that he would join us in a short while. I would have
loved him to turn on with hash, but a short time
passed before the smoking actually began and he had
not come upstairs, nor could we any longer see him
through the window outside. Was he off again? I knew
the girl he was with had her own apartment in the
West Village, and I knew that she was already living
with some fellow; Ernie certainly didn't know this.
Was his first disappearance merely a first attempt? Was
he still determined to seduce that polite girl who obviously did not wish to wound a middle-aged man's
pride, but would do so if necessary? It seemed to me
that he was cruising for bruising. I delighted guiltlessly
in that I had not had the opportunity to warn him.

I wanted to know why Ellen had quit college, why
she was a waitress instead of a wife, why she was not a
hippie and why she seemed so unhappy. What she
wanted to tell me was of a rebuff she had received
from a boy she was sleeping with and of her emotional
reaction. She wanted me to explain why men were that
way. I couldn't. I couldn't explain why women were
that way either. I couldn't tell her anything she wanted
to hear or be anything she wanted to be with—not
even a good replica of a parent to strike out at. After a
while she grew terribly fidgety, especially after talking
about her musician friend, whom she had fought with
earlier that day because he had told her that he wanted
to be left alone, although he was with a crowd of people at the time. In retaliation she had told him that he
wouldn't find her at home when he dropped by later.
Now she wanted to look for him.

"Listen, you want to go to any of the clubs?" she
asked me.

When I said I didn't, she talked a bit about how she
was going to have it out with him.

Then she said suddenly: "Hey listen, I've really got
to go somewhere and be by myself. You don't mind,

do you? Do me a favor and tell Jane I'll call her later."

And then she was gone, off to find the boy who had wanted to be alone.

After everyone in the apartment but myself was stoned we withdrew to the living room to listen to some records and trade in non sequiturs. I perched myself on the arm of a broken sofa near the window and cast agitated glances to the street at irregular intervals. After a while we all became restless and it seemed time to leave. It was after midnight; David had to meet a girl at twelve-thirty and Willard and I were simply tired. David left first; Willard and I left ten minutes after him, during which time we negotiated whether or not to have ice cream sundaes before we went back uptown. Being high, Willard was persistent in his desire for ice cream and I understandingly submitted; I was, however, anxious to get back to see if Ernie was in bed and to see if he was in bed alone.

I sat there for a while, thinking about Ellen and her problems and wondering about her future. Then as I stood up to head upstairs, I realized that I didn't know Jane's last name and wouldn't be able to find the apartment. I also realized that I was very tired and that I had an early and very important appointment the next morning, so I went home, taking satisfaction in the conjecture I would cause by not showing up again that evening. The flower, which I had taken out of my shirt, I left on the stoop for Richie to find. A nice touch, I thought.

The cab ride uptown was about the same as the cab ride downtown had been. I had gone to the East Village trying to meet a hippie and instead I met myself coming and going. In discussing this all with Richie the next day, he suggested that maybe I did meet a hippie and didn't know it. But how can you call a nice Jewish girl from the Bronx a hippie? Or was he talking about me?

When I finally got back to the apartment the suspense surrounding Ernie's adventure had become so much a part of the evening that I was reluctant to end it without savoring the last few taut moments: I looked for clues before I entered the apartment: Was the door open? Was it locked? Was it single- or double-locked? It was single-locked, the way it usually is. I then decided my game was ridiculous and I confidently entered the apartment. Without hesitating one moment, not even bothering to remove my sandals, usually my first response to a carpeted floor, I walked directly toward Ernie's bedroom. The door was closed; I opened it and peered into the darkness. I opened the door wider, allowing the light of the hall to diffuse delicately through the room; under no circumstances did I wish to awaken Ernie, even if he were alone. There was a great, snarled lump sprawled along the vertical axis of the double bed. I still could not tell if that was just Ernie or a couple in a slumber embrace; it is not often that I spy on my sleeping uncle and I had no sense of his proportion to the bed, besides which the girl was rather petite.

When I was convinced that he was single in the double bed I removed myself in tired victory to my own bedroom. But my sleep missed the comfort of total conceit since I continued to wonder what had occurred between the time Ernie left the East Village apartment stoop and returned to his apartment.

I didn't see him the next morning. As I found out later he had an early business appointment and he did not wish to awaken me, as he often does before he leaves. That evening we finally confronted each other but not without a certain shyness, or perhaps embarrassment. Nothing had happened with the girl. After Ernie's crucial and succinct confession, the ambiguity of my feelings resolved themselves in disappointment and relief. I strained to contain the relief and dissembled a most casual, almost literary disappointment in hearing the details of Ernie's chaste evening. I offered suggestions of how I would have dealt with the girl and pointed out the imperfections of Ernie's technique. I explained very simply that he had lost his cool; he had allowed the girl to make him into an accessible image of her parents; he had probably talked too authoritatively and listened too sympathetically. The intrigue of anonymity was dissipated as Ernie leveled about himself with the girl. He played it straight as a middle-aged parent and middle-class businessman; if my forty-two-year-old uncle was going to try to seduce my twenty-year-old girlfriends he ought to have been more subtle in his approach. After hearing his description of the evening I couldn't help feeling that things would have worked out much differently if he had reread with greater care some of the pages in his own book. But, of course, if things had been different my very married uncle couldn't have written about them.

At various times this past summer I had begun to feel that Ernie and I were neutralizing each other. Simply in growing more familiar as roommates, we were beginning to relate to each other more as discrete individuals rather than as symbols of our respective generations. My greatest fear was that any generational opposition would be translated into terms of personal idiosyncrasy and resolved merely by a more generous tolerance of each other's preferences and habits. We realized rather early that we had to be patient with each other if we were to find out what we were each about. But there was a danger that the book was becoming too overpowering as a third force, as a referee; it was becoming the medium of mutual accommodation which was absorbing and homogenizing our differences rather than serving as an instrument of analysis. Alarmed as I was, I could not resist the easy comfort of Ernie's company under the protective shade of our book. And yet the more I enjoyed his friendly company, the greater grew my anxiety that our response to each other had gone flat. I was becoming less interested in writing about my experiences and more interested in just sharing them with my new middle-aged friend. For a while it seemed as if our book was over before we had finished writing it.

Our willingness to write about each other at a distance seemed to indicate the degree to which we had become immune to each other's presence. And yet writing apart from each other turned out to be a most unnourishing meal for our book. I realized this while visiting friends in Maine and vacationing from my uncle's company. After being away for about a week I felt that I could no longer continue writing in a memory vacuum. I was attempting to resurrect previous experiences which had been left unwritten, but the best I could do was to reflect upon them without being able to recreate their immediacy. What I had drawn from those lived moments in the way of vital insight, expressed retrospectively, came out as a most pedestrian philosophy riddled with sociological clichés. I was amazed at how instantaneously "life-felt" shifted into the past tense and how difficult it was to renew its pulse with words.

Writing about past experience is like eating stale bread: you can sop it in soup, toast it, or grind it into crumbs, but there is still no comparison with a warm, freshly baked loaf. Eventually you begin to throw away the stale bread, deciding that the pleasure of saving it isn't worth the trouble of having to prepare it. An alternative to the memory vacuum, the tedious process of etching over the faded outlines of almost forgotten details, is a retreat into pure imagination. But in this book I could not permit myself that retreat without having first paid tribute to the data of experience; otherwise the book would become fiction, not as literature, but as a lie; the very premise of the work disallowed any digression into the sphere of fictional literature. Often I would feel terribly confined in my writing and yearn to explode the claustrophobic reality about which I had to write. I recall my wish while I was away from Ernie to write a lyric celebrating my book or a fanciful short story about the process of writing it. I would have done anything to distract myself from the plaguing requirement of truthful expression, even if it meant irresponsibly discarding material of great potential relevance to our theme.

When I returned to New York Ernie had returned from Fire Island. To sustain the earlier pace of our writing, I now knew we would have to stay together and spark each other's presence more than we had been doing; we would have to recarbonate the experiences that had gone flat and write about our new experiences before they fizzled away.

I called Ernie in his office the day I returned, with all this in mind. On the other end of the receiver I heard Ernie's driest voice inform me that he was going back to Fire Island that evening (a Tuesday) and in the same breath that we had better get moving on our writing since the manuscript deadline was approaching. In light of what I had been thinking, Ernie's statement seemed to threaten any satisfactory completion of the book. Ernie had righteously established himself as the conscience of this book and the conscience of my summer, but I began to see that he also liked to take vacations.

I didn't have time to explain my concern about the state of the book and the state of our relationship. Instead I simply invited myself out to the Island from Thursday on through the weekend. I was determined to assert my presence in Ernie's life and agitate our relationship in the process. On the phone Ernie mentioned that he had been vigorously grinding out pages while I was away. Without even reading those pages I got the feeling that Ernie had begun to write a different kind of book. Why was it that he had so little difficulty writing without me around while I was so constrained by his absence? He mentioned further that he had been philosophizing, and with that confession I grew even more suspicious of what he had been up to. I was afraid not that Ernie had lost the thread of meaning in the labyrinth of experiences (it could be retrieved) but that he had found an improper short cut to the end of the book. I had detected a note of impatience in his talk of deadlines at the beginning of our telephone conversation.

I arrived at Fire Island under a drizzling sky which coincided nicely with my general mood. For the past several days I had been depressed. The newspapers were calling attention to the decay of our country and the ravages of a mindless President. My personal environment tends to become the emotional content of my private life when I am in such a vulnerable mood; everything about me seemed very grave. My sense of humor had become senile by the time this tense summer was waning and I was very impatient for the new challenges of September and the commencing academic year.

But when I saw Ernie again after our extended separation my difficult mood was shattered and I was ignited with new enthusiasm to complete our summer's work; the vision of a finished book patterned my disparate thoughts like a magnetic field ordering scattered iron filings.

Speaking to Ernie for only a few minutes reminded me of things I had neglected to write about and gave me other new ideas to develop. And Ernie became equally anxious to reveal what he had written during the past few days.

One bit of Ernie's material focused on my parents' stay at Fire Island the preceding weekend. My mother had displayed a keen interest in our book and Ernie was openly willing to explain to her some of what we had been writing about. He taunted her by saying that she might be surprised by several of the things she would read; after my mother's arrogant retort that "nothing" her son could do would surprise her, Ernie casually dropped the remark that I smoke pot. My mother was unequivocally distressed by that report. I had intended to have her find out about it when she read the published book and then I would have discussed the matter with her. But Ernie intruded between my mother and me and usurped my prerogative to reveal this delicate information. For no reason that I could easily articulate I felt a seething hostility toward my uncle disproportionate to his manifest deed; actually he had simplified the whole issue by telling my mother from his more respectable position about the harmlessness and even the virtues of pot.

Last week Richie went to Maine to visit friends for

a few days. And at Fire Island, my wife and I entertained his mother, my sister, and his father, my brother-in-law. Naturally we discussed their son, my nephew.

Richie's mother is an intellectually curious but modest woman, a few years older than I, whom the depression beat down and out of the chance to really grow. Naturally she was curious about our book. I told her that she might be shocked at some of what she reads.

"Nothing shocks me any more about Ricky," she told me. "He's been doing as he pleases since he was sixteen. And after all, I read some very sophisticated books."

"Would you be surprised to learn that he smokes pot?" I asked. I knew she didn't know, because Richie had told me. It was a perverse thing for me to do. I am quite fond of my sister. Also, I am aware of Richie's penchant for personal privacy. Yet I had told on him. At the same time I had wiped out my sister's complacency. It would have been revealed in the book anyway, and perhaps this was more kindly than Richie's way. But still, as soon as I said it I was sorry, especially when I saw my sister's stricken look. "Does he smoke pot?" she asked, now very unsure of herself since we were no longer talking about sex, as she had thought. "You know that's one thing I don't like. That worries me."

My sister looked as though I had just told her that Richie had contracted a social disease. So I told her it was no worse than a bad cold. "Well, you know Richie, he has to try things at least once," I lied, still wondering why I had said anything in the first place. "And, you know, it's really very harmless. You'll see when you read about it." Though I really don't know if she will see, or if it is harmless.

All this time Richie's father was very quiet. He never tries to outguess his son, who seems to live on a different planet. He's just proud of him and says things like "that little bastard will be going to school for the rest of his life. When I used to preach to him about an education, I didn't know he was going to listen to me so carefully." Richie's father is a fine carpenter with no formal education. With Richie's crowd that makes him pretty "in."

I doubt if I will be "in" with my son's crowd. He's almost thirteen now. He has a passion for sailing. I'm told he does very well. Last weekend he wanted me to see just how well he can do. I wanted very much to see it. But when he sails with me, even though he really knows more than I do, he gets all goofed up. Isn't that awful? You can bet I'll pay for that someday. My adorable daughter of nine begs me to play games with her. I try, but I soon become bored and say "no more now." That too will cost. I can't help it.

My own father, now seventy-two, who came from The Old Country, was never "in" with me. But when people talk about a good man they're talking about my father. He called me yesterday and asked just one little favor, something he wanted me to do for somebody else and therefore for him. It would interfere with my privacy, but not much. I couldn't do it. Why is that? He just wanted me to show off for him a little. There are so many other things I would like to do for him, but he won't let me.

The question in my mind is who's revolting against whom? I look around and see only that my conformity is different from my father's, Richie's is different from mine. That's all. My father crossed an ocean to run away from home. I crossed from Brooklyn to Manhattan. In some ways it was a longer journey. Richie left home when he was fourteen. His parents thought he was still there, but he had gone and has traveled farther than I. Matthew, my son of almost thirteen, who never wanted to be sent away to camp, now tells us he is very interested in going either to camp or on a student tour next summer. So long, Matthew.

I broke away from my parents while I was still quite young, and I often feel as though I missed my chance

for "adolescent rebellion." There was no struggle and
no authority to rebel against; I just "cut out." Through
much of high school, from the ages of fourteen
through sixteen, I spent most of my time living with
Ernie and his wife at their apartment in Greenwich
Village (it was much more convenient for me, since I
was going to high school in Manhattan as well as the
fact that I enjoyed staying in the Village). Ernie and
his wife never tried to assume parental authority and
my willfulness, strengthened by my distance, weakened
my parents' control over me; I did pretty much what I
liked. When I was seventeen, I began my sophomore
year in college; after spending almost four months in
Europe the summer following my freshman year I
could only think in terms of having my own apartment
when the second year of college began. Throughout
the next three years of college I had scholarships for
tuition and worked usually between twenty and thirty
hours a week to support myself; with the freedom of
complete financial independence and the mobility of
having my own apartment from the age of seventeen
my parents lost their last handle on me. My relationship with them has steadily improved since that time.
What used to be a cordial and rather abrupt relationship has become more intimate; I have found in my
own way a respect for them as individuals and a sincere appreciation of their concern for me as their son.

But I still find it awkwardly difficult and even embarrassing to relate directly to my father and mother as
parents; I relate to them as though I lived on some
ironic cloud; I never face them without the masque of
my accomplishments. Those accomplishments have
consistently given them a sense of pride and I cast that
pride back in their own faces as I use it to barrier my
real self from them. A crisis is precipitated whenever
that hovering mist of pride dissolves and I am left im-
ageless and bare; such was the crisis when Ernie pre-
maturely revealed to my parents that their radiantly
wonderful son occasionally smokes pot.

The more I pushed to break away from my parents,

the more they've stepped out of the way; I've come to appreciate that as the bravest thing they've ever done for me. But they cannot understand breaking the law as anything but gratuitous rebellion. Although I love to shock my parents, to stir them from their parental complacency, I've always attempted to avoid the aspect of rebellion in my actions by propagandizing the angle of constructive independence. Unfortunately, my parents do not understand that to challenge a law an individual must often break it; and even when their respect for the absolute authority of the law is lessened by the many obvious contradictions between what is and what is decreed, they cannot see why *their* son has to be the individual who is going to do the challenging. My parents are the kind of people, like the majority of people in New York City, who would vote against a proposed board of civilians set up to review the actions of the police. They refuse to tamper with authority not because of their implicit faith in its justness but because they don't want the responsibility of scrutiny and the burden of authority placed upon themselves.

My confrontation with the draft has been another instance where I have had to consider doing some challenging. Against my parents' "better judgment" I have had to reckon with the possibility of leaving the country in order to avoid complicity with the perverted war machine that is breathing death in Southeast Asia. It is a very painful thought to have to leave my home and friends, but it seems to be becoming more and more of a moral imperative as I am drawn closer and closer to an involvement in that despised war. But I still don't know if I could really expatriate myself; it is such a permanent and final decision. Always such decisions seem as if they can be postponed or evaded by some other possibility; however, that may be no more than an adolescent fantasy. It is possible that becoming an adult precisely entails such critical decisions; perhaps all the minor challenges to authority so far have been no more than baby steps in preparation for one difficult leap.

After I was reclassified 1-A by my draft board I sent in a request for an appeal, but the board never got around to scheduling a hearing for me; even bureaucracies must slacken their pace for the summer. It is almost September and for nearly two months now I have been kept hanging with no word one way or the other from the board. Of course they cannot draft me until they act on my appeal, but they can and have immobilized me psychologically by agonizingly extending their suspenseful no-response.

Basically I am against the very idea of conscription; in light of the atrocious war in Vietnam conscription becomes a compounded evil. Because the draft is a recognized institution in this country, many distressing problems have arisen with respect to the current war. Of course, as is usual in this country, the cycle of social inequality is flagrantly perpetuated by the blanket deferments given those who can afford to be students or who have achieved the status meriting an occupational deferment. At Columbia there was raging indignation over this deferment policy (apart from considerations one way or another about the war). In a spirit of genuine nobility (perhaps spurred by a collective sense of guilt) a majority of students jeopardized their own deferments by voting in a University-wide referendum not to have class rank released to the draft board. With no other basis for discrimination among students, technically the draft boards could take anyone at any time from the school. I vigorously supported this program of noncooperation with the draft system and the University for once decided to respect the wish of the students by not releasing the discriminatory statistics.

Ironically, in my last year at Columbia College (preceding this summer) I had grades of all As for both semesters and I certainly would have figured at the top in class ranking. A few weeks after graduation I received notification that my student deferment, which would have allowed me to continue in graduate school, had been revoked. I cannot determine whether or not my rank in the senior class would have affected this reclassification, but it certainly would not have been a disadvantage for me if the board had known about it. In a way I was pleased to feel that I had made what had now become a tangible sacrifice in supporting the call not to release rank. But that didn't help my personal situation. True, if I were drafted, sent to Vietnam and killed, some undeferred Negro or Puerto Rican might be spared. And yet that was not the intended purpose of our move to do away with student deferments. No one should have to fight in Vietnam, and by making students as vulnerable to the draft as young colored janitors, the burden of direct involvement in, and responsibility for, the war was being placed more firmly on the no-longer-slippery shoulders of the middle class. Many mothers and fathers with a politically indifferent attitude would have to begin to think about the war in a new context as it became a real threat to the wellbeing of their babies in college.

Well, I believe strongly in the idea of equality (even before the eyes of the draft) and desire more than anything to have peace in the world (particularly in Southeast Asia). But what has happened is that I have been equalized without the war having been ended. My program of draft resistance may end with a bang—in Vietnam. Although I have thought about all the time I could spend reading I know I would not like to go to jail for refusing to cooperate with the draft. And it is becoming increasingly difficult to certify one's self as a conscientious objector (mainly because these days there is so much conscientiously to object to). If my student deferment is not restored upon appeal I will either have to serve in the Armed Forces and demolish the moral principles I hold most passionately or leave this country. I cannot see myself spending the rest of my life in Canada; if I leave I will want to get away as far as possible from the bloodied reach of this country's war mentality. I don't know where I'll go. I don't know if I'll go. The only thing I have decided so far is that I will not kill. At this point, I have no idea of what is going to happen to me.

I hope that by the time my own son reaches Richie's age the kids will have stopped believing their own publicity. Right now, and for a long time, they have been good copy. They have been shills for the national media, the movie industry, the fashion industry, and of course the ad business.

Their creativity has been raped. Their rebellion has been bastardized. They have been egged into self-destructive overstatement.

Everybody seems interested in what they have to say, so they have to find things to say.

Everybody wants in on their fads, dances, dress, so new and more extreme gimmicks must be invented and given meaning. Some of it is great. Much of it is garbage. But they're giving the public what it wants in return for what we gave them. We gave them the gift of affluence, the pill, and education. We also gave them the bomb and a world in revolt. Solve it, kid! We gave them the illusion of power, publicized out of all proportion. Power? Most of them aren't even old enough to vote yet. What kind of power is that?

Educators see them as brainpower. Industry sees them as manpower. Ad men see them as buying power. Still, kids like Richie have no political power and no real economic power. No wonder Richie wants to change the system. No wonder there is student support for every *anti* cause. The only power they have is the power of numbers and of protest.

And because their protest has become so strident, so indiscriminate, so obviously protest for protest's sake, those who are really in power are finding it harder and harder to understand. The louder the protests become, the deafer become the authorities. Even the two burning issues of our day, Vietnam and civil rights, have become obscured rather than clarified by irresponsible overprotest.

And when the kids protest against the authoritarian absurdities of our society, the protests are even more absurd. I've been subjected to the protest of the absurd every time Richie makes a case against me for offenses I have never committed. At the same time my careful if not always successful efforts to be objective and not to overreact become in themselves offensive to Richie.

My friends who live with teen-age "monsters" tell me that their children have a positive genius for always hitting where it hurts most—right in the middle of their parents' self-image. Anybody who wants to understand one of the causes for the Negro riots in so-called model cities need only take a look at a rebellious kid in one of those so-called model families. I think the riots have been incited less by police brutality than by those who keep telling the Negro how much he's doing for him while at the same time saying, "Now, why can't you be more like me? I know that's what you really want."

Keep telling your kid to take a haircut for his own good and watch his hair grow longer. Pretty soon the kid convinces himself that there really is some virtue in long hair. And you become equally convinced that his refusal to take a haircut is a sinister threat to your entire way of life. Richie taught me to understand this, and now that I do it's bugging the hell out of him.

Before I went out to Fire Island for those few days, my mother phoned me in the city. She told me about her weekend at the Island and about Ernie's discussion of our book. She then said, in the pointed tone of maternal irony, "I hear I'm going to be very surprised by some of the things in your book; Ernie tells me that you're a real hippie." I parried her remarks with a brusque "That's right" and announced that I did not wish to discuss the matter any further at the present time. I then sustained an imperious conversation for two awkward minutes and hung up. I knew I would probably never discuss the matter any further.

While working on the first hundred pages of this book I had from time to time wondered how I could relevantly involve my parents in what I was writing. Although my parents were outside the scope of my exclusive relationship with my uncle, I did at least want to mention that I had a pair and give them the immortal pleasure of seeing themselves acknowledged in print (the next best thing to being on television). But I was ultimately able to avoid the necessity of some genteel contrivance. I must thank Ernest for taking the matter out of my hands.

In the wake of this tender episode with my parents (particularly my mother) I was struck by a new realization about my uncle. I arrived at Fire Island and discussed with him the piece he had written about pot and my parents; he admitted that telling them when he did and in the way he did concealed an unredeemably vicious intention. He was ostensibly punishing my mother for her smug pride in her son, but no one had delegated to him such authority. It was sibling rivalry in action that stirred Ernie's venom. As the younger and prettier of two children my uncle was always favored over my mother by my grandparents. I can't help feeling that when he lashes out at my mother, as he often does, he is impelled by this sibling guilt, wishing to destroy its cause. To see Ernie's savage infantile hang-up enacted on such a subdued adult stage is by itself a lesson in repression. Ernie is a fiercely competitive man and it was a curious spectacle to behold the source of that competitiveness cast in psychological relief. I would have hardly believed that my forty-two-year-old uncle could still be psyched-out by his older sister.

As a postscript to the telephone conversation I had

with my mother, I would like to add a note on a subsequent verbal exchange which occurred a week and a half later. I was visiting with my parents over part of the Labor Day weekend while my sister was at Fire Island, probably being interrogated by Ernie. I spent a pleasant Sunday with both of them and planned to return to my apartment the next morning. My mother was leaving in a few days to visit her cousin in California with a stopover in Mexico. All of Sunday I had refrained from mentioning our previous conversation, and although we discussed the progress of my book the subject of pot did not come up; but as I was about to leave, wishing her a good trip (this was the last time I would speak to her until she returned in about three weeks), she asked me if there was anything I'd like her to bring back from Mexico. I replied with wholesome sincerity that, yes, I would love a kilo of Acapulco Gold. She didn't understand, so I explained that Acapulco Gold is the finest marijuana grown on this continent; I also reconsidered my request and assured her that I would be more than content if she brought back even an ounce. She protested slightly. I decided to pursue the issue from an economic angle and pointed out that in Mexico pot is cheaper by the ounce than perfume is in France and lasts just as long; also, I added, there are no duties on it at the border regardless of how much you bring back to the States. Unfortunately my mother was still less than cooperative; some people won't listen to reason.

While trying to convince my mother about the souvenir I so desired, I let drop a few incriminating remarks about taking pot. She made it aggressively clear that she was turned off by pot; but then I brought Ernie's testimonial into the discussion and my mother's invective was mellowed by her respect for the authority of his status and yearly income. I was finally drawing interest on the pot I had invested in Ernie's lungs. As my mother retreated from her initial disdain I became heady with proselytizing passion. I said I'd love to turn her on and my father as well. She then explained that it was not the pot that she objected to most of all, but the things associated with it like hippies and *long hair*. At last I knew we were back to the one issue that has destroyed all happiness for Mother ever since my infant pate began to sprout: my long hair—the blackness in Mother's azure life, the invidious threat to her bourgeois dream. Everything would be all right if only I consented to a monthly haircut; even a trim would renew her vision of my destiny and restore her faith in my future, or at least this is the feeling I get when Mother stings me with her Oedipal pleas; she can become a veritable guilt gun. But I've finally learned to shield myself with laughter every time she makes her bald request.

Finally my mother stated her terms. She said that she would try pot when I got a haircut and looked like "a decent human being." That would prove to her that you can smoke pot and be respectable at the same time. Of course I couldn't accept her sly deal; it would be too much of a sacrifice to cut my hair, and I don't want a Pyrrhic victory. I grinned and told her that she was asking the impossible. We then traded in some playful sarcasms until she thought I had decided to drop the issue; but actually I was calculating the number of months it would take to get Mother to try pot on my own terms. That would be one of my goals for the next year. Of course I am not excluding my father from this program of corruption; the fact is that he is a carpenter, a sensitive man who creates with his hands as well as his head, and I think he is a more vulnerable target and therefore less of a challenge than my devious mother. But by the end of next year I expect I will have turned them both on; perhaps I'll even have them turning each other on.

Almost everything I've seen and heard this summer makes me sure of one thing: the so-called sexual revolution isn't what it's cracked up to be. Understandably, I've been having a terrible time trying to write about sex, but so is Richie. We've discussed it hour after hour, and I still don't see where he's so different or more enlightened that I am, or has so much more freedom than I did at his age. In fact, sexual freedom for most kids, according to what Richie tells me, may start earlier, but it also ends earlier.

Of course, the pill has brought about a lot more opportunity for daughters temporarily to share in the premarital sex life that had previously been an exclusive privilege of sons. Although I and my old Brooklyn buddies must have been sleeping with somebody's daughters. How's this for a frightening thought: Whoever those girls were, some of them are grandmothers by this time. Back in those good old days, their parents could pretend not to know. These days daughters discuss sex openly with their mothers and fathers. It's a fun way for a sixteen-year-old to protest, always good for a laugh, especially since most of us are so envious. We claim to be worried about the kids hurting themselves, veneral disease and all that. Is this what really bothers us? Or do we think that maybe we missed out on something, born too soon for the pill?

I asked Richie about the pill and he tells me that all the girls he knows use it; that as a result they have taken responsibility for not becoming pregnant instead of expecting the boy to use precautions, and this is a change.

Does all this mean that we are raising a generation of loose women? Not at all. Casual as the girls seem to be, and as young as they now become women, they still are women emotionally, and they still cling to the notion of romantic love. All that brave talk about sex being just another bodily function is their little lie.

When Richie and his friends talk about sex to me, all I get from it is that the girls who once only let you touch it, to use the euphemisms of my youth, now go all the way. But the dear young things are still sold on monogamy as a way of life.

The guys resent this possessiveness, as all men do,

yet have little to say about it. They are torn and confused, as all men are, between the need to build within society and the need to exercise their male prerogatives. If the girls are confused, it's not for long. They know what they want. Their only question is how to get it without selling out to their mothers.

So what we end up with is a bunch of kids living together, playing house like we never played house. But if you care to remember, premarital intercourse was not so unusual for engaged couples of our generation. And many an engagement broke up. We also used to talk a lot about trial marriages that they were experimenting with in Sweden. Some of us thought it was a pretty good idea. So now we have trial marriages in this country, many of which turn out to be real marriages.

The kids don't call them trial marriages, they call them relationships. And when they break up there's a lot of heartbreak. It's like a divorce with all the emotional complications, if not the legal and financial ones.

In living together these boys and girls seek and find a kind of domesticity they need. As Richie says, it's like being in a family where you're completely understood. Richie's friends even look for girls who can cook. One of my nephew's friends who has been living with the same girl for three years will soon be married to her.

The other day he was visiting at our apartment and saw the photographs of my children. He started asking questions about them. "How old is the boy? How old is the girl? Do you have any problems with them? Do they go to private schools?" Then he said, "If my sixteen-year-old daughter was screwing around I'd be sore as hell. About my son, I wouldn't care." Another young unmarried couple who had invited me into their apartment were discussing religion. "I think I'd want my son bar-mitzvahed," said the boy, who was Jewish. "I didn't know you felt that way," said the girl, who was not Jewish. "That's awfully nice." And she poured the espresso into our cups.

Richie feels that because kids start experimenting with sex sooner, the girls ask for and the boys expect to give commitments sooner. The younger the kids the shorter the duration of these affairs. The older kids stay serious longer. There's a high degree of faithfulness, jealousy, a lot of side affairs, et cetera and et cetera, all the things their parents have. It's also Richie's guess that all of this will result in earlier marriages. Better marriages? He can't guess.

He still doesn't know how I can be married to the same woman for eighteen years. He has a man's natural yen for variety and for freedom while at the same time feeling a strong emotional tie to one girl. He wants to know how other men, long-married men, work it out. It's not easy.

Men don't tell other men much. They'll admit to neither faithfulness nor faithlessness.

Women point the finger of scorn at other women who indulge in sexual adventures. Most men just mind their own business and read their *Playboy* magazines.

I told Richie "The story, my boy, is as old as prostitution."

"Do you know any prostitutes?" he wanted to know.

"Socially or otherwise?" I asked.

"Seriously," he said, "the idea of having a woman without making any commitment is very exciting to me, very appealing." He went on to tell me of how in Paris and in London, when he was there last year, he had been tempted, but he really couldn't afford the price.

Before the conversation ended he had made the point several times that it would be a very good experience for the book. And I agreed to stake him to the price of a walk up one of the streets in the West 50s that is notorious for its ladies.

"I hope you don't mind going alone," I told him. "I'm interested in publishing a book and not my divorce papers."

Then I told Richie a few things I had never told anybody else. And he told me a few things, too. And I told him a few more things. And we talked, not as men do, but as children, naked and innocent.

And Richie said: "Do you realize what is happening? This is fantastic. Can you imagine a father and son talking this way to each other? It would be too fantastic."

Thinking of my own children, I agree with Richie. Unfortunately, it would be too fantastic.

An event that I had been looking forward to all summer, the wedding of my friend Willard, took place during the second week of September. For three of the four years that Willard was in college he had, most of the time, been living with Sarah, the girl he just married. The wedding was a happy fulfillment of their long affair but did not mean a very marked change in their way of life. Of course their psychological landscape will begin to look different and their recently expanded financial resources will now be combined, but the major revision will occur in everyone else's attitude toward their new status. After college, especially the summer before beginning graduate study, visions of the end of student life and the commencement of "real life" become material possibilities; for some reason "real life" seems to entail married domesticity. Perhaps being a bachelor of arts is enough.

Willard and Sarah have been the first of my close friends to legalize what has been up to now only a tentatively shared life. The finality of their decision has become an uncomfortably symbolic weight pressing on my own thoughts about marriage, and the wedding itself was something like the end parenthesis of my entire rambling summer.

About half of my friends in college have had or still have arrangements similar to that of Sarah and Willard. A girl will often maintain her own apartment (usually with roommates) but it is primarily used as a friendly retreat, for its extra closet and book space, and as a suitable address for mail; the girl will prefer to live with her lover. This removes the difficult tension of separation after a relationship has matured and is the only way of truly knowing the person one thinks one loves. Being awakened in the morning by the warmth of a girl seems to improve one's attitude toward school; the delight in watching her prepare familiar coffee seems to encourage better grades. Living with a girl is simply another aspect of coeducation. And love is the purest experience of learning.

There is a girl with whom I am in love. She has known Sarah even longer than I have known Willard, and when we began our relationship they became our friends as a couple as much as we were all friends individually. At the beginning of the summer my girlfriend painfully departed for a year to study medieval epic literature in Iceland; she had won a prestigious traveling fellowship after graduating with me from college. Not only did this brutally disrupt my emotions and alter my way of life but it destroyed the social pattern we had established with our now-married friends. I could not avoid fantasizing their wedding to be my own; but at the wedding I suffered for the absence of my girlfriend as much as I had wished for her presence. I felt closer to the reality of being married but more distant from the person to whom I would be married. And all that remained for me in the wake of Willard's wedding were questions and doubts about my own readiness to seize stability and contract a fairly permanent marital commitment. It seems so much easier to just continue living with a girl. I suppose I won't be able to understand being married until I am.

The one aspect of marriage that I personally find most frightening is the demand of sexual fidelity; perhaps more accurately it is fear of the guilt aroused by infidelity. For a man monogamy is necessarily a kind of emasculation, but the psychological sacrifice is hopefully rewarded by a rich emotional harvest. Obviously, the critical question is when to make the sacrifice and for whom to make it. In living with a girl out of wedlock you can test your conviction and practice marital fidelity without being condemned to it. The commitment of both partners to each other in this kind of relationship is just as firm and just as "virtuous" as in any ideal marriage; the difference is that when such a provisional relationship becomes less than satisfactory it can be ended without legal complications. Since there is no external bond holding the two people together, both must make a genuine effort to sustain the relationship or else it will simply dissolve.

This summer my sense of experimental fidelity has enforced a kind of emotional frigidity, if not sexual continence. It would be ridiculous and impossible for me to restrain myself from having sex with other girls while I am unmarried and not even engaged. My girlfriend understands this and her decision to go away for a year acknowledges the inevitability of my sexual needs and the necessity of fulfilling them with other girls. But no matter what happens during the year, we will attempt to continue our relationship when she returns. I feel more certain of this after the several sexual experiences I have had this summer. In each case there has been plenty of physical passion but no thaw of emotions; those special feelings are still frozen and stored away somewhere in Iceland.

The most convenient sexual situation is the one-night stand. There is the thrill of seduction (often lost in a relationship) with no sense of obligation and no promise of a return engagement; the girl's attitude is most often the same; usually she does not even insist on spending the night. A good time is had by all. And birth-control pills have simplified everything. With one instant-girl this summer, I did happen to find myself in a continuing affair. After three weekends I realized that I could no longer be sexually intimate without at least hinting at some intimacy of feeling; I knew I did not have such feeling and so I abruptly stopped seeing her.

An issue came up with her which I adamantly refused to discuss: my girlfriend. She had begun to talk about her old boyfriend. But I did not want to involve the girl I love in a similar discussion where the details of our relationship would have to be articulated in the past tense. And I did not want to equate conversationally what is to me the sanctity of love with the profanity of a temporary sexual affair; they are matters of different weight and not to be exchanged even in talk.

The only situation all summer in which I felt any emotional defrost occurred at Fire Island, where I went to escape over a weekend the continuity of my three-week affair. There was a discothèque dance at the town's community hall the evening I arrived and I decided to go, mainly to see the stroboscopic light show. For several minutes I had been staring into space, sweeping with my eyes the room and the people as they flickered in the fractured light; the music seemed to be bombarding the air with every freshly luminous pulse. Then with a smile and a wave a cute little girl weighted down by long blonde hair broke my unfocused gaze. We danced together the rest of the evening.

Walking her home, I learned that she was seventeen.

The next evening as we were walking toward the beach she confessed that she was only fourteen. In fact she had been thirteen just five days before. For some reason I was not astounded; I knew she looked young, but I also knew that I could not tell by looks the difference between a girl three years younger than myself and a girl six years younger than myself; I barely look eighteen, although I'm almost twenty-one. In a way I exaggerated my genuinely cool response to her revelation; I liked her very much, I thought she was very intelligent (particularly if she were only fourteen), and I absolutely did not wish to discomfit her or myself by even slightly reacting. I casually suggested that we continue walking toward the beach and she agreed in an easy breath.

I was somewhat thrilled to be with a girl to whom I was almost seven years a senior. I have regularly gone out with girls of my own age or older and this was a delicious treat; it was flattering to be called the oldest fellow with whom she had ever gone out. Never before have I thought of myself as the oldest anything. As we continued our stroll toward the desolate beach I felt some kind of uncanny relief, like closing my eyes and having a headache disappear. This virginal girl presented no sexual challenge and was no feminine threat; I had no worry of her resistance because my compulsion to seduce her had happily dissolved. I could sit on the shore with her and softly attempt to discover where the black sky began and black ocean ended; I could healthily enjoy her company in the innocent darkness and talk as an equal to a girl three years younger than my "kid" sister. I had nothing to lose by exposing my mind.

We talked about love and girls and my girlfriend; we talked about pot and parties and high school. I was delighted to learn that she too was an artist and just about to try out for the High School of Music and Art, from which I had graduated some four years before. As we continued to chat I found myself responding to her with greater candor and greater ease. For the first time all summer I was being honest with a girl about my feelings and I found that for the first time all summer I was talking to a girl for whom I had some feelings.

Of course we kissed; she may have had more experience than I wanted to believe (that certainly marked a change in my attitude) but I resisted the impulse to go beyond what my lips would allow. When I left her, my feelings about seeing her in the city were very ambiguous. Apart from my projected ill-ease in dealing with her parents I was very wary of my own self-deceiving vision of this pretty young girl; it wasn't only that I felt like a dirty old man. Thinking in terms of my distant girlfriend and my proclaimed emotional fidelity, I realized that this fourteen-year-old girl was as dangerous to that fidelity as I wanted to believe she was safe.

My manifest reaction to Willard's wedding must have been caused by some kind of psychic implosion; there were many highly energized latent thoughts orbiting around that critical event. I had been having dreams of anxiety in anticipation of the occasion and in mentioning them to the prospective groom I observed that his anxiety was less than mine. Much of this distress I expect had to do also with the end of the summer and the strain of completing this book. Ernie had already finished his writing and the rest of the work was left to me. I was paralyzed with concern over what I could write as a suitable ending, and in that mood the wedding took on symbolic significance.

The wedding reception was held at a beach house near the tip of Long Island. Some friends of mine were driving out there from the city and I went along with them. We arrived at the house in the late afternoon and Willard greeted us almost as soon as we stepped out of the car. An official ceremony had taken place earlier (it was just for the family) on the edge of the cliff, and now the wedding party was beginning on the lawn in front of the house; there was a huge yellow-and-white tent erected next to the house and inside it almost a hundred bottles of excellent French champagne were being opened for a fewer number of guests. The whole place seemed like a summer camp on the weekend when all the parents come up to visit.

The groom was attired in black denim slacks from the House of Wrangler and wearing a permanently unpressed open-collared shirt created for him by Monsieur Van Heusen; it was half untucked from his pants. Then I saw Sarah smiling quizzically in her colorfully embroidered whitish muslin shift with a huge circular diamond hung like a pendulum around her bare neck. Her neck was also supporting a pendant of heavily tangled gold-leafed wire that occasionally clanged against the diamond; it was a handmade gift from one of her parents' artist friends and I liked it very much; it looked the sculptured version of a Jackson Pollock painting.

Wearing a suit, I felt as if I were in costume, although my sandals and sockless feet were not out of place. I quickly went back to the car and exchanged my white shirt, suit jacket, and wide tie for that favorite striped polo shirt I stole from my uncle; I had brought it along because, knowing Willard, I had expected some kind of rustic scene. All the guests had stripped down from what even originally seemed to be less than formal attire and all were delighting in the comfortable incongruity of a casual wedding party; as far as I am concerned it's the only kind to have. The champagne was being opened as if it were Pepsi-Cola, and everyone was barefoot.

In a paroxysm of happiness Willard sputtered that now his friends had arrived and the party could really begin. As we stood around waiting to greet a few other people, I couldn't help feeling like a kid. I felt as if I were at some grown-up persons' wedding, friends of my parents or of my aunt and uncle; I could not believe that the bride and bridegroom were actually friends of my own. After all, they were only kids like me.

But at the same time I felt that Willard and Sarah had deserted the "younger generation" by getting married, going off and becoming "adults." I used the term *younger generation* as I jokingly expressed my feeling to Willard only because he knew of my attitude toward what I was writing and understood the term as my signal of sarcasm. All the same, he became suddenly very distressed as if I had momentarily reawakened his own fear of the solemnness of being married. Although my remark was made frivolously I did feel that the sobering truth could not be giggled over and Willard was weighed down by what I had said. I then quickly smashed our mood by assuring him and myself that he really hadn't become an adult and Sarah zigzagged over toward us in a way that seemed to confirm my words; she assertively stammered that it was positively ridiculous for us to think of ourselves as adults. And so we all made a burst for the champagne to hurriedly celebrate the certainty that we were all still kids.

The summer is over. Our book is over. Last night Richie and I tried to work toward a conclusion.

We sat in my bedroom with the air-conditioner whirring, drinking Seven-Up and eating donuts, and we cut our manuscript to pieces until my bed was littered with scraps of typewritten pages. Then, with a stapler, we spliced our story together again. As we worked and argued about what should follow what, we grew mind-weary with ideas that intermingled and kept spawning litters of new little ideas. It was almost as though we could now start the book anew. I realized then that this one is endless. It will just stop because we will stop writing when my family returns in a week and Richie moves out.

Tonight I offered to buy us a steak dinner in celebration of the fact that all that is left for us is to put the finishing touches on our manuscript. I am still wary of Richie's reaction to my businessman's taste in restaurants, so I suggested a casual and relatively inexpensive place in the Village, The Tin Angel. We sat on a balcony one flight up, overlooking a busy Bleecker Street. We ate escargots, mopping up the garlicky sauce with thick chunks of brown bread. The beer was cold and the steins were comfortably heavy in our hands. When our sirloin came it was thick, juicy, and rare. We lingered over espresso and, in the mood of the mild evening, talked of royalties and fame and felt the foolish pride of the well-fed. In this state of secure wellbeing, neither of us was disturbed in the least, as we had been on our last visit, by the teeny-bopper-ish tawdriness of the West Village scene below.

Having finished our meal, we strolled west up Bleecker to Macdougal Street, and then north, stop-ping every few steps to window-shop.

Richie wanted to buy a wedding gift for his friends who had just been married. I wasn't too sure of what he was looking for until he steered me down some stairs into a little headshop.

As we looked around, a very friendly young lady be-hind a counter asked me "Are you his father?"

"No, I'm not," I answered.

"What makes you think we're related?" Richie asked.

"I don't know, just the way you act with each other," the girl said.

"That's fantastic," Richie said. "He's my uncle."

Turning to me and with a movement of her head that took in the entire store, the girl said, "Do you know what this is all about?"

I smiled and said "Yes, I do."

"That's nice. My mother was here to visit me and she didn't understand what anything we sell was for."

"I turned my uncle on," Richie told her proudly.

"That really is nice."

"Yes, it is," Richie said, peering into the showcase. "I was wondering, I want to get a gift for a couple who have just been married. Would this hookah with the two mouthpieces be appropriate? Or do you think two of these glass water pipes would be better?"

"Oh, for a newly married couple, I think something they can smoke together would be lovely," said the saleslady.

"But they've been living together for three years." Richie argued for the little glass water pipes, which he clearly favored.

"Well, in that case," said the girl, "a set of individ-ual water pipes would be very appropriate."

For almost two minutes Richie said nothing; he just kept looking back and forth between the glass pipes in the case and the hookah on the shelf, as though weighing his decision. Then he remembered to ask the price. "How much?"—pointing only to the glass water pipes.

"Five dollars each."

"I'll take them," Richie said decisively as though he knew he had found a bargain.

"Oh, say, one thing I forgot to tell you," said the girl. "We don't gift-wrap."

Gift-wrapped or not, no wedding present that Richie's young friends receive will have been chosen with more forethought or promise of pleasurable fulfillment. And surely there will be no duplicates unless the bride is registered at some other headshop.

Of course, my nephew had also given me a gift, another lesson in the lore of the young. In theory he should have learned more than I this summer, but if he has, he isn't saying.

I've even learned to imitate his style of writing and I amused myself with it recently when he showed up at the beach some days ago, resentful because I had taken a short vacation just when he felt he needed me for the book. A week earlier, he had breezed off to Maine, almost in the middle of a sentence, seemingly without a care or a qualm.

Having sneaked a peek at his notes, I know he was annoyed with me because I had been writing ahead of him and had been pressuring him on the deadlines. To tease him, I wrote this slick copywriter's parody:

> My uncle would like me to discipline myself to work and play at his fox-trot tempo, but the boring metronome beat of Ernie's nine-to-five, five-day-week existence lulls me into a stupor and leaves me as empty-minded as the music of the forties.
>
> A thought dropped into the stream of consciousness is like a pebble dropped into a pond. The ripples must be allowed to expand to their ultimate end before another pebble is permitted to fall. Typical of his generation, Ernie carries pebbles by the

handful and impatiently throws them one after the other destroying the subtle ripples of thought by drowning them in new ripples before they reach the maturity of the shore.

In Maine, where the water is wide and deep and where I can create my own ripples, I will minutely examine each vibration while my impetuous rock-throwing uncle splashes words on paper without piety or pause for reflection.

It is true that Richie takes great care with what he puts on paper, while I prefer to shoot first and ask questions later. But now he is working furiously to convert his notes into a proper finish for this book. It's almost as though he wants the last word.

The fact is neither of us will have the last word. This was made quite clear to me by Richie's sixteen-year-old sister, who graced my Fire Island home over the Labor Day weekend. And there too were my son, my little daughter, and their friends, all proving to me that there is no last word for us to write.

There were five or six teen-agers on the wide wooden deck lounging around when my wife and I and our guests came off the beach.

A friend of mine pleasantly asked a sixteen-year-old girl why she was wearing a decorative bell hung around her neck on a long leather thong: "Is that so your mother knows where you're at?"

She answered just as pleasantly: "That's so *I* know where I'm at." And then she added "I'm not a hippie or anything. I'm just goofing on people."

"Goofing on people? What does that mean?" I asked her.

"Well, you know," she said. "Sort of kidding; you know, making fun of people, but not in a mean way. Like making them think I'm a hippie or something, because I wear a bell. I'm always goofing on my parents, and anyway I like the sound it makes."

We adults sat in the sun, sipping our drinks, and the kids with Coke cans in hand proceeded to enlighten us about pot, protest, and the pill. The women didn't want to hear of marijuana or peace marches. So the kids told us about sex.

"If I listened to my parents and wait for my wedding night I'm liable to marry the first schnook that comes along," said a pretty friend of my nephew's sister.

"But you're only sixteen," one of the women said.

And the girl answered: "To you I'm sixteen, but to me I'm *sixteen*."

Just as I was about to fall madly in love with that girl for that remark I was distracted by the arrival of my son Matthew and one of his twelve-year-old friends.

I said, "We're talking about teen-agers. Maybe you'd like to hear this."

"What for?" said Matthew.

"We know it all already," said his friend, Freddy.

"Well, maybe you want to come out here and help us," said one of the older kids.

"Why should we help you? You've never done anything for us," said Matthew's friend.

"You're the older generation," said Matthew.

"Four years isn't a generation," said a seventeen-year-old boy.

"That's by your line of reasoning," said my thirteen-year-old.

The seventeen-year-old smiled a sickly smile. But I laughed right out loud.

Exit Ernie laughing at the new generation. Soon enough they'll be hip old has-beens, complaining about the dumb kids who think they know everything but secretly suspecting that maybe the dumb kids really do.

Ernie's family has returned to the apartment in the city. But for the existence of our manuscript it could easily seem as though our summer never existed. It is already dissolving into a dream and the dream into an echo. On the stage we had occupied for three summer months a new show is being enacted; it is now the regular season and something like a family situation comedy has returned to the apartment just as those shows return to September television. As I am eased out of Ernie's home and family life, I return to my own new apartment and prepare to begin graduate study.

Ernie opened this book and I have requested to close it. I have, however, for several weeks resisted writing my conclusion. It is possible that I do not want this book to be finished; in fact, it may be that I do not want it to exist at all. For reasons that I think are implicit throughout my writing, I began our summer endeavor with doubts and reservations about the kind of book this might turn out to be. Ernie's material dominated the first half of our manuscript mainly because I was slow to become enthused with the project; he had been the one to come up with the initial idea. But as the summer progressed I did become enthused and involved and I soon found almost too much to say. Part of the difficulty in writing a conclusion is selecting among so many unwritten thoughts.

I finally did write a conclusion but it will not appear in print.

The pressure of an ending summer had become an unbearable strain; I found myself unable to motivate my

125

pen. I felt choked by my commitment to complete this book. At the same time I became hostile toward my uncle. In a gasp of desperation I seized one concrete issue, my disagreement with Ernie over the choice of a title, and for almost twenty pages I sustained a verbal tantrum directed at my uncle's "commercialism," and concluded by expressing consummate disappointment about the book. With an attitude of diffidence verging on shame I presented the final piece of writing to my uncle's eager eyes. He was noticeably shaken, not so much because of what I had written as by why I had written it. When I handed it to him I had sheepishly said, "No hard feelings"; that was my way of cluing him in to the reaction I really wanted while at the same time sincerely meaning what I said. His indignant anger after reading it was largely a response to the many truthless distortions I had venomously nurtured; his pity was a response to the ridiculous spectacle I was making of myself.

My first reaction to his dismay was practically a total retraction of everything I had labored to put on paper; I stated that I was not sure I wanted to use the piece I had just written. It then became clear to him as well as to me that I had written such a seething conclusion for the sake of a reprimand. My relief told me that I was correct. Only by a harsh, almost parental rebuke could I ultimately define myself with respect to my uncle.

The book was practically done. In one summer my uncle had penetrated my "exclusive insularity." My feelings were oscillating between delight at his understanding and outrage at his invasion. To have ended the book sweetly would have jarred the balance. I needed a logical structure for my irrational anger; I invented some details and exaggerated others in an attempt to mold my raging feelings into a discursive form.

As the summer progressed my uncle learned more and more about me; it finally got to the point that almost nothing I did could provoke his censure. It wasn't that he approved of everything, but he had most viciously learned to refuse to condemn. All of my attempts to force my uncle into a neat parental package had failed; I could not get him to perform his middle-aged authoritarian role. I began to think of him as a martyr of enlightenment, but more interested in being martyred than enlightened. And his canonization was made possible only by the destruction of my adolescent ego.

Ernie condemned me for what I had written. He said he could not allow me to make a fool of myself. He said he would not permit me to use such a conclusion. As he was speaking I knew there was no longer any need for me to use it.

We had then lived through what was unquestionably the end of our book and the end of our summer. In my own painful way I demanded that he become once again only my uncle. He complied for one satisfying moment.

We left the bar in which we had been sitting. Ernie paid for the two beers. On Broadway he summoned a cab. Upon entering the apartment I received benevolent greetings from my aunt and cousins. Dinner was almost ready.

In the cab Ernie and I had had a friendly chat. Going up in the elevator Ernie decided that we ought to turn on his wife, my aunt.

I had welcomed with relief the chill of an autumn evening as we got out of the cab.

New American Review 1 2 3 4

In its first year of publication, NAR has established itself as the bold new voice of American writing. Each issue of this paperback periodical contains more than 250 pages of fiction, essays, and poetry that speak to the issues of American experience here and now. NAR has been hailed as "the best of the literary journals" (*The Commonweal*) and as "a vital dialogue between public concern and private imagination." (*Book World*) Here are some of the reasons why:

NEW AMERICAN REVIEW #1
Fiction by William H. Gass, Grace Paley, Philip Roth; Stanley Kauffman on his experiences as drama critic for *The New York Times;* Richard Gilman on "MacBird and its Audience," "Burke and Marx" by Conor Cruise O'Brien.   (#Q3254—95¢)

NEW AMERICAN REVIEW #2
Fiction by Allen Friedman, E. L. Doctorow, Edward Hoagland, and John Barth; poetry by Günter Grass; essays by Nat Hentoff, Neil Compton and Staughton Lynd.   (#Q3365—95¢)

NEW AMERICAN REVIEW #3
Featuring Philip Roth's "Civilization and Its Discontents." Other fiction by R. V. Cassill and Donald Barthelme; essays by Josephine Herbst, George Dennison, and Frank Kermode.
                          (#Y3455—$1.25)

NEW AMERICAN REVIEW #4
An emphasis on politics and political criticism featuring Robert Coover's "The Cat in the Hat for President." Other pieces by Eric Bentley, Conor Cruise O'Brien and Mordecai Richler.
                          (#Y3562—$1.25)

THE NEW AMERICAN LIBRARY, INC., P.O. Box 2310, Grand Central Station, New York, New York 10017

Please send me the SIGNET BOOKS I have checked above. I am enclosing $_____(check or money order—no currency or C.O.D.'s). Please include the list price plus 10¢ a copy to cover mailing costs. (New York City residents add 5% Sales Tax. Other New York State residents add 2% plus any local sales or use taxes.)

Name_____

Address_____

City_____State_____Zip Code_____
Allow at least 3 weeks for delivery